D0949169

DEATH
IN THE
TETONS

Eddie "Cola" Fitzgerald's Last 24 Hours

Susan Tatarsky

Copyright 2014 Susan Tatarsky

All Rights Reserved

ISBN: 0985924543

ISBN: 978-0-9859245-4-6

E-book: 978-0-9859245-5-3

Library of Congress Control Number: 2014915109

Qi Note, Incorporated

Canadensis, PA

Author's Preface

This book is based on over three years of investigating the events leading to Eddie "Cola" Fitzgerald's death.

The Fitzgerald family initiated a wrongful death lawsuit against all of the entities they considered to have contributed to his death. This suit was settled in late 2012. The settlement details remain confidential.

Hundreds of man hours were spent by investigators and expert witnesses to ascertain the facts of the incident. Thousands of pages of depositions were taken from members of the Long Island Ski Group, the Targhee Ski Patrol and members of the Teton County, Wyoming Sheriff's Office/Search and Rescue volunteers and members of the Teton County Idaho Sheriff's Office/Search and Rescue volunteers. It is estimated that out-of-pocket expenses to investigate the case were $200,000.

Eddie Fitzgerald's death received extensive media coverage from Oregon to New York, both in print and broadcast media. The story was picked up on the Internet and on many blogs. Interest has been broad, but until now the specifics of the incident have been purely speculation, innuendo and personal opinion. Many writers on the ski blogs immediately assumed Eddie had been "poaching powder," a term that describes skiers intentionally skiing out of bounds to find untracked powder snow that can provide the exhilarating sensation of skiing on velvet.

Before he was found unconscious, Eddie had been skiing at Grand Targhee Resort. In resort skiing, skiers are expected to follow marked trails within the confines of a patrolled ski area. He was scheduled to take a 4 p.m. bus back to Jackson Hole with the other members of the Long Island Ski Group. His first attempted 911 call was at 3:54 p.m., indicating he knew he was lost and was trying to notify authorities.

In the style of a *roman a clef*, I have changed the names of all the characters except for the Fitzgerald family. Each character corresponds to a real-life person. The facts presented herein are untouched otherwise. I have created dialogue based on interviews with these and other persons, and legal testimony gathered in the process of the lawsuit. With the goal of constructing a narrative of these last hours in Eddie "Cola" Fitzgerald's life, I have taken the liberty of creating additional dialogue and thoughts of the persons involved.

All statements in bold italicized quotes are extracted directly from testimonies as recorded by the legal stenographer. (Please note that in these testimonies, as well as the Introduction, the names are changed to reflect the names of the characters in the narrative.) Italicized text without quotation marks indicates my own renditions of the thoughts of the characters.

Acknowledgements

Many thanks to the following individuals who contributed their time and knowledge to make this book possible:

Gil Barreto
Dave Bender
Aaron Dunn
Attorney Roy A. Jacobson
Jackie Rybee
Hope Strong
Brian Terry
Writers in Transition, Cuenca, Ecuador

I also wish to acknowledge my editor, Franny Hogg Lochow, whose expertise was invaluable to this project.

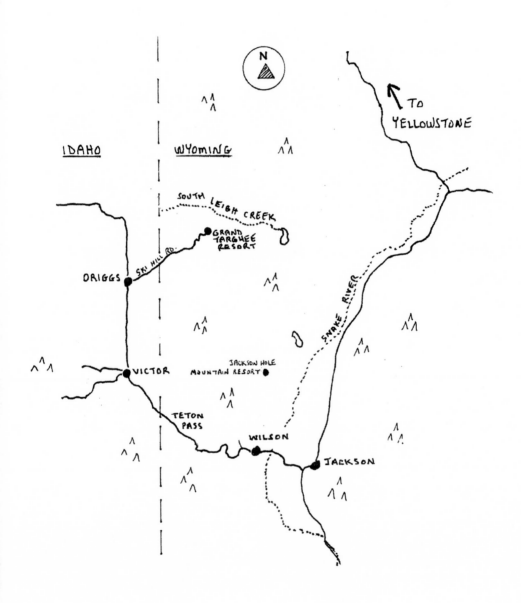

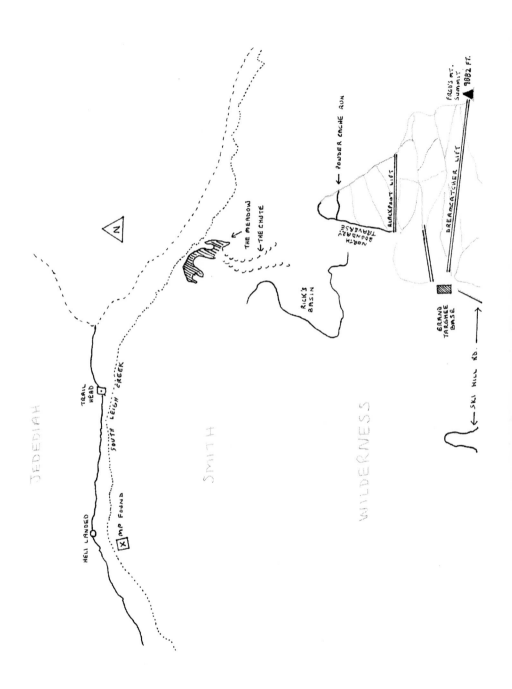

Table of Contents

Introduction

BY ED FITZGERALD SR.

The date was January 20, 2010. My girlfriend Carla and I were on a ski trip to Copper Mountain, Colorado. This was our third visit to Copper. On the first one, we stayed in the small town of Frisco, located seven miles from Copper and an ideal place for skiers to stay who wanted to split their time between Copper, Breckenridge, Keystone and Arapahoe Basin. Frisco was a town of approximately 3,000 people consisting of condos, private homes, small shopping centers and restaurants. A typical mountain town with an elevation of 9,000 feet. Our second trip to Copper we stayed on the mountain proper. The base of Copper, one of the highest in the Rockies, is 9700 feet. We weren't ready for that altitude and both of us suffered from high altitude sickness, i.e., headaches, dizziness, insomnia, etc. We learned our lesson from that experience and on this visit we prepared ourselves by hydrating with a liter of water daily. It worked and up until the 20th, this trip was a huge success.

While Carla and I were in Colorado, my 46 year old son Eddie was skiing with his Long Island ski group at Jackson Hole, Wyoming. At 5:30 on that evening, the phone in the condo rang. Carla picked it up and said: "Ed, it's for you. It's Gail."

Gail is my ex-wife and the fact that she was calling me from New York almost paralyzed me. This could not be good news. I got on the phone and she said "Ed, it's about Eddie. He was skiing in Wyoming and got lost. They found him this morning and he had died from hypothermia."

I dropped the phone and started screaming "Don't tell me that... don't tell me that ... don't tell me that" ... as if by repeating it, this horrendous fact would evaporate. I returned to the phone and said "Gail, oh my God...what happened?"

She said "We don't have the details, but apparently he was skiing alone and got lost. They didn't find him until this morning." I told her we would be coming back to New York as fast as we could and that I would call her as soon as I got there. I asked her if our daughter Christine was with her and she told me she was. We hung up, and I looked at Carla...stunned, devastated and unsure of how we would get through this.

The next day, January 21st, we drove the two hours from Copper Mountain to the Denver airport, my mind was spinning all along. How could Eddie get lost skiing at a ski resort? This was not back country skiing—Eddie didn't do that. He and his friends skied virtually every weekend throughout the entire winter and took annual trips to multiple ski resorts throughout Europe, Canada and the Western U.S. He had never gotten lost, never gotten hurt, never required assistance of any kind from ski patrols or search and rescue teams.

When we landed in New York, Gail filled me in on some of the details of the trip. Eddie's group had taken a day trip from Jackson Hole to Grand Targhee, located about 40 miles north of Jackson Hole, a much more benign and smaller mountain than Jackson Hole but known for its vast amount of powder. Actually, Targhee was considered a respite from Jackson Hole—a "day off" from the intense skiing Jackson is noted for, and a mountain with only three major lifts and restricted terrain.

Gail had made preparations for Eddie to have a memorial service to be held at the Fox Funeral Home in Forest Hills. She and Christine arranged for Eddie's remains to be cremated in Wyoming and to be brought to New York by Ted Knowlton, one of the leaders of the Long Island ski trip. I concurred with this decision and the ceremony was scheduled to take place on January 25th. Nearly one hundred of Eddie's friends showed up at the memorial service. One of them told Christine that the ski group "blew it" when they had not done a head count on the bus before returning to Jackson Hole after the day's skiing at Targhee. Halfway through the memorial service, Gail handed me a note from Anna Gustafson, a reporter from the Forest Hills Ledger. The note said that she had important information about Eddie's death in Wyoming. I called Anna the next day, and she said she had a friend who worked for a newspaper in Idaho who claimed there was something fishy about the story about Eddie's rescue efforts.

The next day I called the editor of The Valley Citizen, located in Driggs, Idaho. (Driggs is just over the state line from Alta, Wyoming, where Grand Targhee is located.) The editor told me that the search for Eddie had been unusual: searching down the mountain from the top rather than from the bottom up since Eddie had made it clear in a series of 911 calls that were communicated to Idaho Search and Rescue, that he was in a meadow by a stream among fallen trees. This description only applied to one area near Targhee and that would have been the South Leigh Canyon. He told me that he had been in touch with the Teton County Wyoming Sheriff, who was responsible for search and rescue. He could only tell me so much because he was having various conversations with Sheriff Jennings, but promised to get back to me as soon as he received more information.

Soon after that, I received a telephone call in New York from Sheriff Jim Jennings. After introducing himself and offering his sympathies, acknowledged that the Wyoming Search and Rescue team had screwed up and made lots of mistakes. Primarily, not having "boots on the ground" and trying to conduct the search from Jackson rather than Targhee. In addition, Jennings said the 911 dispatcher, Mark Silver, failed to communicate the substance of Eddie's three 911 calls which were received between 7:30 and 7:45 p.m. This was hard to understand, since Jennings also told me that Idaho SAR was having a training session in a room adjacent to that of the 911 operator and could have monitored the 911 calls. Idaho SAR, located in Driggs, was only a couple of miles removed from where Eddie's 911 calls were originating. Jennings told me that Eddie had been flown to St. John's Hospital in Jackson the morning of January 20th and was treated by the emergency room doctor, Dr. Steeler.

The next day I talked to Dr. Steeler who told me Eddie was brought in at approximately 11:30 a.m. and that he was hypothermic and unresponsive. He also told me he had been found in South Leigh Canyon. I asked him why he thought Eddie would have gone there, and he said it was unintentional, because nobody skied into the South Leigh Canyon without "skins," and on that day it was snowing intermittently and the visibility was poor.

Dr. Steeler had requested that SAR transport Eddie to EIRMC (the Eastern Idaho Regional Medical Center, located in Idaho Falls, approximately 70 miles from Jackson), where there was a trauma center fully equipped to administer to accident victims. Apparently weather precluded this and St. John's tried to resuscitate Eddie, performing CPR for an hour and a half. Initially, they had some reason for hope but in the final analysis, they could not revive him.

Dr. Steeler gave me the name of the person responsible for Wyoming SAR, Don Oscar, as well as his telephone number.

I called Don Oscar who is the paid SAR coordinator working in the Teton County Wyoming Sheriff's Department. When I got through to him I asked if he could tell me what happened to Eddie. He told me Eddie was skiing in an intermediate area (the trail map indicates all the trails in this area are identified as diamonds or expert trails).

Oscar told me Eddie skied out of bounds by "ducking a rope." In other words, that my son intentionally skied out of bounds. I asked him why Eddie would do this and his response was, "he was looking for powder." Since I was unfamiliar with the Grand Targhee Ski Resort and the Powder Cache run Eddie had been skiing, I mentally visualized the rope running parallel to the trail and indicating where the out of bounds area was. I asked Oscar that if Eddie ducked such a rope to find powder skiing, why wouldn't he just ski along the trail on the out of bounds side, and then duck back under it so that he could go back inbounds. Oscar then told me that in fact Eddie skied in a perpendicular line away from the trail and that he descended a steep "chute" into the Sough Leigh Canyon, that he followed a snowmobile track and then got lost.

After this discussion with Oscar, I decided to call Sprint to determine if Eddie had placed any other calls on his cell phone. Sprint reported that Eddie had made seven 911 calls that day, at 3:54 PM 4:05 PM, 4:25PM, 5:35PM, 7:32PM, 7:34PM and 7:38PM. Only the last three calls got through to the 911 dispatcher. Since Eddie had been scheduled to return to Jackson at 4 p.m., he was obviously attempting to notify people he was lost at that time. He could not have been "looking for powder." Furthermore, it was subsequently found out that in fact, there was no rope for Eddie to duck when he went out of bounds.

Based upon these preliminary findings—multiple 911 calls had been made, and the story we were being told didn't make sense—the Fitzgerald family decided to investigate, bringing a wrongful death lawsuit against the responsible parties. This was done soon after we made these discoveries. The complete story follows.

—Ed Fitzgerald, Sr.

Chapter 1
A New Yorker In Wyoming

"Eddie could tell you the capital of any city, any country, the topography. When he would travel someplace, he would know exactly where he was at all times." —Ed Fitzgerald, Sr.

It seemed to Eddie "Cola" Fitzgerald that the sound of his awkward steps through the deep snow, post-holing in his ski boots while dragging his skis behind him, was the loudest thing he'd ever heard. He kept going. He was sure he must be near a road, it was just too dark to see.

Hours ago he had skied the fall line down the mountain—the natural path of travel—as he'd done hundreds of times in his life while skiing all over Europe and North America. He'd been expecting to find a traverse—a trail that would lead back to the base village of Grand Targhee. If there was one, he hadn't spotted it. Nor had he seen any signs indicating the resort boundary. No wonder, though—in the snow and fog, visibility had been terrible.

It felt odd to be alone like this, at night, in the woods. Even the times he had gone camping with Fred, there had always been other people around. Lost? That had never happened to him in his life! But he couldn't think about that now. The temperature was falling and he had to get out of here.

The cellphone had worn itself out looking for a signal and was almost out of power when one bar began to flicker at the top of the screen. He had already reached the dispatcher twice, briefly, before being cut off. Surely they could track his signal and figure out where he was. And the ski group must have noticed his absence by this time and alerted someone. Yes, they were probably out looking for him right now.

The stars were out. The sky had cleared at last, and it wasn't snowing anymore, but he shivered in the January night as he stood holding his phone with reddened fingers, gloves held between his knees. He pressed the three numbers again and held the phone to his ear.

"Nine one one. Where is your emergency?"

"This is Edward. Do you know where I am?"

"Uh, Edward."

"Yes."

"I need you to tell me what kind of GPS unit you have. Do you know, is it one that gives you a latitude longitude, or is it a beacon or is it a UTM?"

Eddie shut his eyes tight. He had told them his phone had a GPS, but he had never used it. He didn't know what a beacon or a UTM was. He opened his eyes. "It measures latitude, I don't know."

"It measures latitude longitude?"

"Yes."

"OK. Do you have it turned on right now?"

"I don't know how it works."

"You don't know how it works? OK. Do you have it out right now?"

END OF TRANSMISSION

* * *

Most New Yorkers don't know where Wyoming is. There's a vague notion of cattle, and rugged men on horseback. Cheese, perhaps—or is that Wisconsin? One imagines Wyoming might have seen action in the Wild West of days of yore, but one is not certain. And doesn't the state's seemingly arbitrary rectangular shape suggest it has few outstanding topographical features that could define its boundaries with any sort of elegance—say, on the order of the Mississippi River, or the Great Lakes?

To a geography-challenged New Yorker, Wyoming is just one of those boxy states you can't tell from Colorado or Utah. One could easily think there's nothing much out there. But one would be wrong, because Wyoming is home to a few hills known as the Rocky Mountains. Mention of them in popular song—

the Rockies may crumble, Gibraltar may
tumble, they're only made of clay,
but Our Love is Here To Stay

or perhaps this popular baby boomer ditty—

You can talk to God
and listen to the casual reply,
Rocky Mountain High

is testament to their iconic status in the land of the free and the home of the brave. Stretching 3000 miles from New Mexico to British Columbia, the Rockies vary in width from 70 to 300 miles. The western two thirds of the State of Wyoming hosts a big 'ol chunk of Rocky Mountain.

Many visitors to Wyoming come there to see Yellowstone, the world's first designated National Park. Inside Yellowstone, in addition to the famous Old Faithful geyser, one can also gaze upon the Continental Divide (the demarcation of drainages running either towards the Atlantic Ocean or the Pacific Ocean) that runs in a northwest-southeast direction through Wyoming's Rockies. It

slices through the lower left corner of the state if you're looking
at it on the map. Now look to the right: the lion's share of the
rectangle was acquired in the 1803 Louisiana Purchase, when the
United States bargained with France for ownership of the Louisiana
Territory. In the west and the south (or left and down), pieces of
the Wyoming Territory created in 1868 were originally owned not
only by France, but also by Mexico, Great Britain, Spain, and the
Republic of Texas!

So, yes, in the history of the Wild Wild West, Wyoming had its
fair share of territorial ambiguity and disputes, especially between
the white American settlers and the indigenous peoples of the
the Great Plains region to the east: Lakota, Crow, Shoshone, Nez
Perce, Flathead, Arapaho, Bannock, Blackfeet, Cheyenne, Gros
Ventre, Sioux, Ute. There may be no more cowboy and Indian
battles but the fighting continues nevertheless. Today it's in the
form of jurisdictional responsibility at Wyoming's western border
with its neighbor, Idaho. Guns and bullets and bows and arrows
have been replaced by that most modern of weapons: red tape.
More on this later.

The name 'Wyoming' doesn't even come from the West,
but from the Wyoming Valley in Pennsylvania. Named by the
Algonquins—who never got further west than Scranton and
Wilkes-Barre—it means 'at the big river flat'. Pennsylvania's Battle
of Wyoming, one of the Revolutionary War's most famous, was
commemorated by Thomas Campbell in his 1809 poem Gertrude
of Wyoming. The poem's popularity is presumed to have inspired
the naming of that remote, rectangle-shaped territory 2000 miles
due west of Pennsylvania. Indeed, it's said that residents of the
area were puzzled when Congress, from their headquarters 1500
miles to the east, bestowed the moniker "Wyoming" on the state
in 1890. (One can imagine the conversations that might have
ensued: "Wyoming? What the heck does that mean?") Back East,
it was such a popular name that New York State also used it for

one of their own towns. The State of Wyoming, however, does not have a town called New York in it.

Some of our legendary folk heroes are associated with Wyoming, the Equality State: Buffalo Bill, Kit Carson, Sacagawea. Butch Cassidy did a stint in a Wyoming jail. And whence the state nickname? It so happens that Wyoming was the first United States territory to grant women the right to vote, in 1869. It was also the first to elect a woman governor: Nellie Tayloe Ross took office in 1925 following the death of her husband, the previous governor. Other judicial areas benefited from this policy of equality, as Wyoming also had the first female jurors, court bailiff, and Justice of the Peace.

The notion of Equality, however, did not extend to those of other races. Battles with Native Americans notwithstanding, an event now known as the 1885 Rock Springs Massacre highlighted the discrepancy in wages and hiring of Chinese versus American miners employed by the Union Pacific Coal Company. Wyoming's wildness bared its fangs again a few years later when the Johnson County War between groups of cattle ranchers erupted. This conflict was documented in the 1980 film Heaven's Gate.

If geography-challenged New Yorkers need additional proof that Wyoming not only exists but has done so for over 140 years, they need only focus ye olde historical telescope on the infamous Teapot Dome Scandal, in which Secretary of the Interior Albert Fall was convicted of taking bribes in an oil reserve leasing deal. If one puts an ear to Interstate 25, rumblings of the Harding Administration grinding to a halt can still be heard. Up until Watergate, it had been the country's worst scandal ever.

So New Yorkers, don't try to deny it—the State of Wyoming has indeed made its mark on history. As far as your average New Yorker is concerned, however, it's a big question mark. What, for instance, is the capital city? Just like Pennsylvania (Philly would be Penna's capital in a heartbeat if she only could), Wyoming's most famous area is not the capital. When Long Island Ski Group leader Fred McKuen announced to members that the next annual trip would be to Wyoming, everyone knew of Jackson Hole, the famous ski area, but no one knew what the state capital was. No one, that is, except 46-year-old Eddie "Cola" Fitzgerald, a postal worker from Queens, New York.

Eddie's diagnosis of a neurological disorder was first made in the 1960's, before autism became the highly prevalent condition—1 in 88 children—that it is today. Thus, he was thus never officially diagnosed as "autistic." Nevertheless, he displayed the characteristics of a high-functioning autistic person. He was highly intelligent, but his lack of conversational skills would have led a stranger to believe he was not very bright. As he reached middle age, his mouth twisted a bit and gave his face a skewed appearance. He was tall and lanky, and naturally uncoordinated—except when he was on skis.

Eddie's need for schedules and routine, and his attention to detail, made his job as a mail carrier the perfect fit. Having attended special schools up until his college years, Eddie yearned to be accepted as a 'normal' person. He strived to continually challenge himself in many areas, both intellectually and physically.

Eddie knew the capital of Wyoming was Cheyenne. He knew all the state capitals. He knew all the world capitals. He had spent a goodly portion of his childhood poring over a huge National Geographic world atlas given to him by his grandfather. He could read and understand maps quite easily. He had a near-photographic memory. These skills did not help him, however, on that fateful day at Grand Targhee Resort in January of 2010 when he failed to see a small sign reading "closed" that was mounted on a bamboo pole as he skied through snow and fog down the fall line of Fred's Mountain.

That tragic chain of events began with a map. Or, to be precise, two maps containing conflicting information. One of the maps was inside the other as an insert. This ski trail map for Grand Targhee Resort was posted both at the bottom of the lifts and printed on a pocket-sized trail map available to patrons. On January 19, 2010 at the top of the Blackfoot chairlift (the last lift Eddie "Cola" Fitzgerald rode), only the insert portion of the map was displayed. While the main map clearly showed the dotted yellow boundary line at the bottom of the Blackfoot lift—a groomed road called the North Boundary Traverse which led back to the base of the resort—neither the insert nor the blowup showed the boundary line. Rather, it clearly indicated that the resort boundary continued along the ridge of Fred's Mountain, past the beginning of the North Boundary Traverse road and down to the bottom of the Nordic skiing area known as Rick's Basin. On this map, no closure was marked. Anyone looking at it would conclude that the entire open slope of the black diamond Powder Cache trail all the way down to Rick's Basin was clear and open for skiing.

In reality, the section in between the North Boundary Traverse and Rick's Basin was a closed area. During the proceedings of the wrongful death suit brought by Eddie's father, even the testimony of Grand Targhee ski patrol personnel in their depositions admitted what the map showed was incorrect. Before being deposed for the lawsuit, none of the patrollers had realized that the map at the top of the Blackfoot lift gave false and misleading information.

No one knows whether or not Eddie Cola looked at this map before he made that last run down Fred's Mountain around 2:30 p.m. or so on January 19, 2010. But as it was his first time skiing at Grand Targhee, and given his familiarity with map-reading, one would imagine that he did. And if he had depended on this map— the last directional indicator he would have seen—there would have been no reason for him to be on the lookout for a closure line at the North Boundary Traverse road. On the contrary, he would have approached it as he would any of the many other traverse roads he would have already encountered while skiing Targhee since 10 a.m. that day. The near-white-out conditions sent most of his fellow ski club members into the lodge. Eddie, though, never passed up a chance to ski. A later examination of his tracks leaving the resort boundary showed that he breezed right over the boundary without stopping, evidently never seeing the "closed" signs on the bamboo poles.

* * *

Skiing and snowboarding are without question among the most expensive sport activities out there. You're talking three figures each just for basic equipment, even for a pair of good goggles. Not to mention lift tickets (which can cost $70 per day at a high-end resort) and lodging, and travel expenses. It's not exactly beyond the means of the middle class, like flying airplanes or owning racehorses, say—but it ain't a cheap date.

Nevertheless, the Long Island Ski Group was a thrifty bunch. The members worked for a living, and not on Wall Street. They called it a group though it had no formal membership. The core of the group was a bunch of friends who lived in the Glen Cove, New York area, but its annual ski trips were open to anyone willing to pay the fee. Its founder, Fred McKuen, had been running the trips since 2003, which gave him the opportunity to ski for free.

The trip to Wyoming in January 2010 was set to take place the week of the Martin Luther King holiday when folks would have the extra day off from work. When it came time to book the hotel reservations, the last place Fred wanted to stay was the pricey Jackson Hole Mountain Resort. Sure, they would ski there. But money was better spent on lift tickets, and food and drink. You're hardly ever in the room anyway. So the more reasonably-priced

Parkway Inn of Jackson Hole was to be the group's headquarters for the week when they flew out of LaGuardia and arrived in Jackson, Wyoming on Saturday, January 16, 2010.

The group's mood at their home airport in New York was festive. The forty-odd New York-based members arrived at LaGuardia before 6 a.m. on Saturday, some by cab, some leaving their cars in the long term parking lot, while others were dropped off by a family member. After going through security they assembled at the gate for United Airlines flight 361 to Jackson.

Ross and Marco, who tended to be inseparable during the ski trips since they were of the same age (early thirties) and similar snowboarding ability, drank coffee and discussed equipment. Ted Knowlton, a fireman in his forties, checked the weather report for Jackson on his Blackberry. Larry Andersson, in his early fifties and still a beginning skier after years of lessons, was searching his carry-on bag for the paperback he thought he had packed. Rich and Cheryl, the newlyweds, held hands as they sat gazing at the TV tuned to CNN, mounted overhead. They were both tall and good looking, and made a cute couple.

"Oh my God," remarked Cheryl. "Do you think they could have the TV on any softer, you can't even hear it."

Rich laughed. "You're only thirty-five, don't tell me you're going deaf already. Anyway, TV is always better with the sound off." He put his arm around her as she snuggled against his shoulder.

Eddie stood near his close friend Fred McKuen, who was discussing the recent film Avatar with Kathryn, another senior member of the LISG. When the conversation drifted to the topic of Fred's new grandson, Eddie looked over Fred's shoulder as he showed Kathryn photos of the baby. As usual, Eddie did not contribute to the conversation, although he always enjoyed listening.

Ted Knowlton, the fireman, walked over to them with his Blackberry and a paperback in his hand.

"Hi Kathryn. Here's your guidebook back, thanks for loaning it to me." He ignored Eddie. "Hey Fred," Ted said, "excuse me, did you say we were skiing Jackson Hole for two days before we go to Grand Targhee?"

"That's right."

"And how far is Targhee from Jackson Hole?"

Fred shrugged. "You mean in miles? I don't know exactly. I think we have to drive over that Teton Pass through the mountains to get there. Eddie probably knows."

"Yeah?" said Ted with a snort. "Never mind. I'll look it up myself."

Eddie's perpetual slightly-twisted smile left him as Ted returned to his seat in the departure lounge, punching keys on his mobile device.

Kathryn patted Eddie's back. "Don't mind him, Eddie. You know he's a grouch. Here." She offered him the Teton guidebook. "Do you want to read this?" Eddie shook his head. He picked up his shoulder bag and looked at the floor as he walked as far away from Ted as he could get.

"Why does Ted have to be so mean to him?" Kathryn asked Fred. "Eddie never did anything to him."

"Who knows? But you don't need to protect him. Eddie Cola's a big boy. He can take care of himself."

"I just don't like how Ted treats him. There's no reason for it," Kathryn said.

"Well, people do things there's no reason for every day." Fred paged through the photo album again before he closed it and tucked it into his knapsack.

The pre-boarding announcement for Flight 361 came over the PA system, and the group began to stuff mobile devices and reading materials into coat pockets and carry-ons. Before long they were onboard, joking and calling out to one another across the aisles.

On the six hour flight to Jackson, Eddie had a window seat, his favorite. He loved to look out at the panorama below, matching what he saw to his knowledge of terrain and geography. In addition to having skied throughout Europe and North America, Eddie had an encyclopedic knowledge of map-reading. Perhaps it was in his genes, being that his dad, Ed Sr., had been an Air Force navigator who flew frequent training missions during the Cold War.

Ed Fitzgerald Sr.: "In May of 1957 I reported to Harlingen Air Force Base, Texas, and attended flight school for one year. I received my navigator wings one year later. Then I was assigned to the 376 Air Refueling Squadron, located at Barksdale Air Force Base in Shreveport LA. After getting checked out on the KC97 (the Air force conversion of the Boeing Stratocruiser Airliner to an aerial tanker) I was assigned to a combat crew, whose mission was to refuel B47 and B52 bombers. Every six months our squadron would fly from Barksdale to Goose Bay Air Force, Labrador (a 10 hour flight) where we would be 'on alert' 24/7 in the event of war with the Soviet Union. Our mission was to refuel either the B47's or B52's on their way to drop their atom bombs on the USSR. In preparation for a possible war we would fly two or three 8 hour training missions weekly from Barksdale. There was always a refueling squadron, and a bomb squadron, 'on alert' throughout the US and Europe. The USSR knew that, and that was what protected us from them in the era prior to the ICBM. The 376 ARS was discontinued in 1963, as the newer, jet engine KC 135 replaced the KC97. The 135 was a conversion of the commercial 707 for military use. I completed active duty in May 1960. So, the war I fought in was the Cold War which basically lasted from the end of World War II to the fall of the Berlin Wall. Few people understand how important the Strategic Air Command was to keeping us safe before missile defense."

Upon landing in Jackson, the heads of the passengers were bowed—not in prayer, but in turning on their cell phones, which now displayed 1 p.m. Mountain Time, two hours earlier than New York. They descended the metal staircase waiting beside the plane, and breathed in the crisp mountain air during the short walk across the tarmac.

The Jackson Hole Airport was surprisingly well-equipped for its size. The waiting area featured comfortable armchairs situated around a large, modern, gas fireplace. There was a restaurant, and several tourist shops. Wood beams, rustic wood paneling and stone were the primary design elements, in keeping with the Nouveau West theme so prevalent in Jackson Hole. The tony ambience of the place was in stark contrast to the actual facilities, which included exactly one tiny luggage belt. The time it took for the belt to make a complete loop was barely enough to nuke your cup of coffee in the microwave.

A long row of stunning nature photographs stretched across the back wall of the room. Rocky Mountain sunrises and sunsets; a bison's head emerging from a swirling snowscape laden with ice crystals. Wolves. A close-up of a mama bear with two cubs. Despite the creature comforts of the airport lounge, there was no mistaking the fact that this was the West, still wild after all these years.

After twenty minutes or so all the ski and boot bags and luggage were unloaded from the belt onto the luggage carts. Then it was time to head out to the group's lodgings in Jackson. On the forty five minute ride to the Parkway Inn, heads turned this way and that to look at the expansive vista in which they were enveloped. (The original airstrip dates back to the 1930s and was located within the boundaries of the Jackson Hole National Monument before the monument and the park were combined. The Jackson Hole Airport is the only U.S. commercial airport to be located inside a National Park.)

Why is it called Jackson Hole? The word 'hole' is an old trapper term referring to the sensation of reaching the valley floor by descending from the steep slopes above. When one enters Jackson Hole (containing the communities Jackson,

Teton Village and Wilson) one enters a basin with walls of mountain all around.

Though the road into town was marked with advisories on moose and elk crossings, no animals were encountered. The ski group members soon found themselves at the corner of Jackson and Deloney where the Parkway Inn is located. Ross and Marco were delighted to find the New York City Subway Shop right across the street, which surely would satisfy any sudden cravings for hometown food.

The Parkway Inn was a quaint, colonial style building situated two blocks from the main square in Jackson Hole. Owner Joanie Ryder, a kind, cultured and attractive woman, loved hosting ski groups because "they're so much fun." She and her daughter Mackenzie took immediate notice of Eddie, who remained off to one side by himself while others in the group congregated in bunches in the well-appointed lobby loaded with antiques.

Joanie: "There was something compelling about him. He stood out."

Eddie had a mascot-like quality that enabled him to be an esteemed part of the group without having a verbal presence. Most people rely upon words when they wish to put others—and themselves—at ease. Eddie did put others at ease, but not with words. Rather, he had a warmth to him, a welcoming and accepting vibe that needed no verbal bolstering. Perhaps he developed this quality as a result of being rejected by his peers as a youngster— but one imagines he could have developed a habit of retreating from human contact instead.

Christine, Eddie's sister: "Eddie was bullied and called a retard by kids in his elementary school. They were very cruel to him. I wish I could have protected him but we went to different schools ... Eddie had one friend when he was around 8 or 9 years old. His name was Jamie Frye. The Fryes moved shortly after he met Jamie, and Eddie was devastated. He closed himself off and didn't allow anyone besides us to get close to him. When he joined the Post Office he found out that there are people out there that he can trust and call a friend. He made many friends at the Post Office. I thank God for that."

Christine recounts the very first time they went skiing, when she and her brother were teenagers. She and Eddie were riding in the car with their father Ed Sr.., when a car accident on the highway caused a major backup.

Christine: "We were trying to go to the Olympics in Lake Placid, it was 1980. I remember saying 'let's go skiing.' I think that was my idea. So we went up to Canada."

The mountain where the Fitzgeralds ended up was Mont Tremblant in Quebec, about a 90-minute drive from Montreal.

Christine: "We rented skis. We had our skis and poles, we were in our jeans and our jackets, snow gloves, and whatever we were wearing. We got on the chairlift and we got up, and we were all in a complete state of panic trying to get down. It was freezing. The three of us picked our way down. People helped us the whole time, like 'look at these Americans in jeans, it's zero degrees out.'"

A non-skier would naturally wonder as to the mental state of people who like to ride a tippy metal bench strung on a wire up to the top of a snow-covered mountain in the freezing cold and slide down it at high speed standing up with their feet attached to a couple pieces of wood. Only skiers know the truth.

Christine: "It was exhilarating. Plus, it was, we don't know how to do this, so we're going to find out how to do it... We got down, and the next thing you know we're taking lessons at Hunter Mountain."

Located in the northern Catskills of New York State, Hunter was the Fitzgerald's home mountain. They went there every weekend for many years. An annual winter vacation would be to Vermont, or better still, back to Mont Tremblant.

Christine: "We liked it there, it was quaint. You didn't have to deal with the Vermont skiers and the New York skiers, 'cause they're pretty obnoxious. Because skiers know that they're doing something that most people can't do. They don't have the gumption or the balls to try it. Or the money."

For the first time in his life, Eddie began to acquire a real skill that not only bolstered his self esteem, but also earned him respect from others. In college, however, Eddie's pursuit of a Bachelor of Science degree in Chemistry took all his attention and energy, and skiing fell by the wayside. But it was in his blood, and Eddie's friend and Postal Service co-worker Fred McKuen got him back on the slopes. He was accepted as an equal by the members of the Long Island Ski Group, who liked Eddie for his friendly personality and respected him for his skiing ability. The fact that he rarely spoke was never held against him. These people may not have had as high an IQ as Eddie had, but he felt comfortable with them.

Fred McKuen, founder of the Long Island Ski Group: "Everybody liked Eddie. He was very easygoing, very honest. He had a good sense of humor for a guy that was quiet. He was always around. If you needed a favor, Eddie was there for you."

* * *

Born in 1963, as a child Eddie showed little interest in the activities that most little boys love. When his father Ed Sr.. tried to play catch with him, Eddie would flinch when the ball approached.

Ed Sr.: "It became obvious that sports requiring a ball were not going to be in Eddie's future."

But long before that first game of catch, Eddie's parents, particularly his mother Gail, had noticed all was not well with this child.

Eddie had been a breech birth. His first act after being born was projectile vomiting in the hospital. He turned out to be a happy toddler, though he was late to speak and to walk. Around the age of seven, it was becoming more and more clear to Ed and

Gail that their son had issues. Concerned, they brought Eddie to Children's Hospital in Boston, where he received a diagnosis of "minimal brain dysfunction and hyperactivity disorder." From there they were referred to Dr. Lee Salk, an expert in neurological disorders. Salk was the brother of Jonas Salk, developer of the polio vaccine. Dr. Salk declared Eddie a "borderline moron." Frustrated with this diagnosis, Ed and Gail determined to learn more about Eddie's mysterious condition that belied what they perceived as his high intelligence.

Had Eddie been diagnosed during the 1990's as opposed to the early 1970's, Asperger's Syndrome would have been suspected immediately given the prevalence of autism in today's children. (One must keep in mind, of course, Asperger's Syndrome is only a recently-discontinued medical label for a pattern of symptoms that includes awkward social interactions, muteness, idiosyncratic speech, physical clumsiness, and over-dependence on schedules and routines—all of which Eddie demonstrated at various times.)

Ed Sr.: *"Because of his difficulties in verbalizing his ideas, Eddie's intellect was often underestimated."*

"Borderline morons" are not usually able to get Bachelor of Science degrees in Chemistry, as Eddie Cola did. But it was true that he was not someone you'd call 'coordinated'. The fact that he was able to attain a high degree of skill in the physically challenging sport of skiing is testament to the tenacity Eddie showed in overcoming the natural awkwardness of his body. As a child, it had taken him many weeks of practice with training wheels to learn how to ride a bike. Even the simple act of crossing the street on foot required him to mentally and physically prepare himself. He had lots of opportunities to practice street-crossing later on, given his job as a mail carrier in Queens, New York, a position he held for twenty years.

Gail, Eddie's mom, had actually gone back to school for child development and education so she could understand Eddie's condition better.

Gail: "My choice of education was necessitated by the fact that I wanted to get the best educational environment for Eddie and this really directed my life... He had a different way of learning. Nobody was tapping into his strengths, they were focusing simply on his weaknesses. I removed him from public school in 2nd grade and put him in a Montessori School for a short time and then started my own non-profit private school. I had a small enrollment of approximately 120 children, ranging from pre-school or nursery school through 6th grade. I opened the school primarily because it was a way for me to help children who, like Eddie, were slightly different as far as their learning styles went. I had very bright children and I had children who were slow. Then he went to another private school that had many of the strengths that I felt I had in my own school. It was a Fidel School in Glen Cove; it's no longer there. Children were given the opportunity to work on their strengths, and there was a great variety of instructional techniques used. He was there for approximately four years. He went to camp there too, during the summer, so there was a continuum of people and techniques."

Eddie then attended high school at Karafin School in Mt. Kisco, a 2.5 hour commute by subway and bus. He was never late. He loved school and was loved by his teachers. Often when the school closed because of snow, he didn't know till he arrived because he had to leave the house so early. He graduated second in his class. He earned his degree in Chemistry from Southampton College and would have loved to become a scientist, but advanced education in that field required more academic ability than Eddie could deliver.

Gail: "He always came at things sideways. There were labels each time he was diagnosed; every year there was a different label. One year I said, my gosh, he started out with 'learning disability' and now they are

*saying 'neurologically impaired' and 'emotionally something or other'.
It just went on and on. The labels were meaningless, I felt. Asperger's
Syndrome did not exist then. I didn't hear about it till I read a book on
Asperger's about five years ago. Some of the symptoms Eddie had: his
attention to detail, his need to have a schedule and to perform the same
way each time."*

Neurologically impaired perhaps, but Eddie "Cola" Fitzgerald
was still a typical New Yorker: tough, feisty, determined, skeptical.
New Yorkers take a lot of things for granted, because anything they
want is right there. If Wyoming folks are defined by the Code of
the West, then New Yorkers might be defined by the Code of The
Best. The Wyoming license plate features a cowboy on a bucking
bronco. The New York license plate features both Niagara Falls
and the Empire State Building. 'Nuff said.

Chapter 2
The Morning Of January 19

"This is the worst day of my life besides my parents dying."
—Fred McKuen, Long Island Ski Group founder

Kris Hart arrived at the Grand Targhee parking lot the morning of January 19, 2010, at 7:40. He had just enough time to get to the boot room by the Papoose conveyor lift for the morning ski patrol meeting. He chugged the dregs of the cup of coffee he had picked up at Pendls in Driggs and gave Andrew, a fellow ski patroller, a friendly punch on the arm as he walked over to the trash can to toss in the empty cup. Mandy was already there, as was Jared, and the other sixteen ski patrollers. Most were wearing their red ski patrol jackets, and several of the younger males in the group sported fledgling mountain man beards.

Jon Alexander walked in and erased the names from yesterday's sweeps off the board. He was acting Ski Patrol Director today as Director Pete Kerry was out of town. "Anybody seen Jesse?" he asked the team.

"He's off today," said Andrew.

"Oh, right," said Jon, turning a page in the log book. Jesse O'Leary was a senior patroller, avalanche expert, and trainer of rescue dogs. He also served on the Teton County Idaho Search and Rescue team.

Bill Redmond, another senior patroller, walked in armed with the day's weather report and the avalanche forecast.

"Whatta we got?" asked Jon.

"Six to twelve inches. Twenty-four to forty-mile-per-hour winds," Bill informed him.

"All right!" several patrollers exclaimed at once.

"Looks like a pow day," said Kris to Andrew, who smiled at the thought of skiing fresh powder while on duty. The fluffy, virgin snow known as powder is a skier or snowboarder's raison d'être. The snow report indicated a mid-mountain settled snow depth of 57 inches, meaning that the powder would settle on top of packed snow on the two mountains at the resort, Peaked Mountain and Fred's Mountain. There are ski patrol posts on each one.

Jon turned back to the board and wrote in the name of a patroller next to each sweep listed, referring to his log book periodically. The sweeps consist of checking the groomed runs for hazards such as piles of snow left from the groomers, rocks or trees sticking out., maintaining rope lines, mountain signs and trail signs. Kris saw his name next to Lift Line for the a.m. sweep, which meant he would be covering the Wandering Moose, South Street and Sweetwater trails, all ungroomed. He'd also be responsible for checking the condition of the Dreamcatcher lift tower pads. Before going out, however, he would be sitting dispatch for an hour. Then for the afternoon sweep he was scheduled for North, which would include checking the North Boundary cat track, a groomed trail that also served as a traverse back to the base.

Kris began writing the summit log, marking the time, date and day and the weather observation at the summit: Temperature—24. Current Wind Speed and Direction—20. Visibility—poor. He began to fill in who was in charge of which sweep. This morning Andrew would handle Quiver sweep. Jared would be over by the

Sacajawea lift patrolling the Powder Reserve Traverse and checking signs and backcountry access gates. There were also several call boxes located at points where guests might need assistance; each of these needed to be checked daily.

Pete Kerry, Ski Patrol Director: "When you're new you're taught the sweep by an experienced patroller. So the experienced patroller goes out and shows you where the signs are, what they should look like, what the spacing should be. Every third bamboo [pole] is roughly what we try to do, every third piece of bamboo has a sign on it."

"Danielle, one of our regulars said there are two signs down along the north boundary, put those back up," said Jon. "Mandy, I need you to check the padding on the Sac lift tower, see if that tear in the cover has gotten worse. And we have a few volunteers joining us today—thanks guys," he said, motioning to two women and two men sitting together in the corner of the room. Volunteers augment the regular patrol by as many as eight people, particularly on weekends. In return for their services they receive season passes but are not paid. Nor are they covered by worker's comp.

After fifteen minutes or so, the patrollers assembled their gear and headed out to the mountain. Some would do morning sweeps, others would check specific spots on the mountain. It was already snowing, and was fairly windy and overcast—a not atypical winter day at Grand Targhee, whose nickname is "Grand Foggy," much to the chagrin of Targhee administration, who don't consider it a compliment.

Grand Targhee Resort is located in Teton County, Wyoming, in the Caribou-Targhee National Forest in Alta. It's 42 miles northwest of Jackson and accessible by road only by way of Driggs, Idaho. It averages 500 inches of snow each season, ranking it among the four top ski resorts in North America as far as powder snow. The nearby Jackson Hole Resort is the star of the show in that area, however. It's larger, the mountains are steeper, and the base village has more lodging, restaurants and stores, making it an ideal destination for the Long Island Ski Group's 2010 annual trip. Not everyone in the group chose to ride over the Teton Pass from Jackson to Targhee, though. Of the fifty four people on the tour, forty eight made this side trip, with two skiers meeting the group at Targhee after staying with friends in the area.

After an intense two days of skiing and snowboarding at Jackson Hole Resort, the group was on a roll. Though many had never been to Targhee before and weren't sure what to expect, Fred had planned it this way on purpose—a midweek side trip to a resort whose verticals are considerably less steep than those of Jackson Hole.

The day got started over at the Parkway Inn at around 6:15 a.m. Rich, Ross and Marco were the first LISG folks to arrive in the breakfast room. A continental spread of juice, muffins, cereal, yogurt, bagels, coffee and tea awaited. Gradually the rest of the group sauntered in, helping themselves to the spread and making space at the small tables as more people showed up. Eddie "Cola" Fitzgerald sat at a table in the corner drinking orange juice and eating a bagel with cream cheese.

"Hey Cola, you ready to pound the powder or what?" said Freddie McKuen, Fred's nephew, sitting down next to Eddie with a cup of coffee and a bowl with cereal and yogurt. (Eddie's nickname was "Cola" because of the fact that, unlike everyone else in the group, he did not drink alcohol.) Eddie smiled and nodded. "Eddie Colaaaaahh!" said Ross, squeezing by the table with empty paper plate in hand, going for seconds. Eddie grinned and looked up at Ross as he passed by.

Ross: "I think I can count on both hands how many words he has said to me in the three years I've known him! But every one of those words has put a smile or a laugh on my face."

Someone asked John, Larry's roommate, if Larry was coming on the trip. "No way. He's still sleeping, even," said John. "What a wimp. He's gonna go shopping or something."

Larry, deep in dreamland as they spoke, was unaware of the side trip to Targhee planned to take place that day. A novice skier but a veteran on the LISG trips, he would go mainly to sightsee and hang out with his friends. This was the day he'd dedicated to his search for an authentic cowboy hat. The Jackson Town Square was a few minutes walk from the Parkway Inn, and he was sure he would score at one of the many shops there. By the time Larry woke up around 9 o'clock, the group going to Targhee was long gone.

An 8 a.m. departure had found them boarding a standard size coach bus and a smaller minivan to go to Alta, about 90 minutes northwest of Jackson. The sun rises later in Wyoming than in New York, and it was just barely light out. A few flurries drifted down, and skies were gray.

"I thought you said it was going to be bluebird today," said Ross to Marco as they sat next to each other on the large bus. "Hey," replied Marco, "who do I look like, Lonnie Quinn?"

"Not even close Dude," said J.R, from the seat behind them, prompting a good bit of laughter at the comparison of the plain-featured Marco with the handsome New York TV weatherman.

The group's other vehicle, the minivan, carried about a dozen of them, plus the gear. Eddie sat by himself in the back and looked out the window. Rich and Cheryl sat a few rows in front of him. "How you feeling honey?" Rich asked his wife, seeing Cheryl rubbing her right calf.

"God, my legs are burning. I mean, I'm going to ski... but I think I'm going to take it a little easy," she sighed. "Yesterday and the day before, that was a lot of skiing."

The previous two days at Jackson Hole Mountain Resort had quite a few in the group rubbing sore leg muscles. At 4,139 vertical feet the slopes are steep and challenging. Good ski areas draw good skiers, and the combination of conditions and camaraderie pushed many in the group to max themselves out each day. Then there was eating, drinking and socializing to be done before crashing out in the hotel room, and waking up the next day to do it all over again. They were grateful for Mackenzie Ryder—daughter of the Parkway Inn's owner—and her rocket-fuel coffee in that large thermos in the Parkway's breakfast room.

Heading west out of Jackson on Rt. 22, they saw more signs warning of moose and elk crossing, and an advisory that no trailers are allowed on Teton Pass, the only land passage across Taylor Mountain. It's a typical mountain pass, full of switchbacks, and thin guardrails on embankments that would total any vehicle/driver/passenger unlucky enough to breech the boundary. The mountain's apex is 8,000 feet. The drivers approached the snow-covered switchbacks with extreme caution; otherwise, their destination might not be Grand Targhee, but the Happy Hunting Grounds.

As the Long Islanders gazed at the gorgeous scenery out the window, they were thankful they were not driving today. Even for a veteran driver the route could be a bit nerve-wracking. The really scary part of the pass lasts about fifteen minutes, then the road levels out onto a plain again, proceeding through the tiny towns of Victor, then Driggs, Idaho. The magnificence of the western plains is evident as Idaho Rt. 33 passes in an endless straight line through winter's browned fields scattered with farm equipment, horses, and the occasional house.

Alta, Wyoming, where Grand Targhee is located, is in Teton County, Wyoming. But remember, it can only be reached by way of Teton County, Idaho. The twin Teton Counties are a rare example of adjacent counties sharing the same name. 911 calls in the vicinity of Alta, Wyoming, are frequently routed to the dispatch in Driggs, Idaho. Because of this situation there was a Memorandum of Agreement in place in 2010, between the Sheriff's Offices of Teton County, Wyoming and Teton County, Idaho.

Sheriff Jim Jennings, Teton County Wyoming: "When a call came in and it was a Search and Rescue incident [from] Teton Valley, Idaho ... [they] would communicate to us what was going on and a plan would be made as to what the response would be."

Section A9, Article II of the MOA in place in 2010 stated the following (with similar wording for Wyoming assisting Idaho): *The Teton County, Idaho Sheriff agrees to assist the Teton County, Wyoming Sheriff in response to emergency Search & Rescue incidents occurring in Teton County, Wyoming, as requested by the Teton County, Wyoming Sheriff, to the extent of available resources, with the understanding that limits on the response provided will vary depending upon the seriousness of the emergency, duration of incident, and distances involved.*

The Long Island Ski Group was completely unaware of the political complications arising from time to time regarding the sharing of resources between the two Teton Counties. There wasn't any reason for them to be aware of it, they were just there on vacation. And what a vacation it was. Even though some of them had been on the prior LISG trip to Jackson in 2004, it was always a delight to be in this beautiful area, so different from not only their home base of New York State, but also from other ski areas they had visited in North America and Europe: Andorra, Spain in 2005; Big Sky in Montana in 2006; in 2007 Innsbruck, Austria; in 2008 Whistler Blackcomb in Canada; in 2009 Taos, New Mexico.

Cheryl was one of the ski group people who had skied with Eddie "Cola" Fitzgerald the most. She met Eddie on the LISG 2003 trip to Courmayeur in the Italian Alps. It had been the first LISG trip for each of them.

Cheryl: "We skied all over the world, camped and hiked in the Adirondacks, lounged around Block Island ... We used to joke with each other that it wasn't a vacation unless we were both there... he was the easiest person to be around."

Cheryl had begun skiing in Vermont in 1999 while she was a student at LeMoyne College in Syracuse and dating a ski instructor. Her father worked with Fred McKuen at the post office, so eventually she began taking part in Fred's annual Long Island Ski Group trips. When she began dating Rich, they would do day trips up to the Catskills, usually Belleayre or Windham. They'd typically leave on a Sunday at 5 a.m., ski for the day, then drive home. Weekend trips were to Sugarbush in Vermont.

Although Cheryl was a veteran, this was her new husband Rich's first LISG trip, and he barely knew Eddie. But Rich had heard from several members of the ski group that even though Eddie didn't talk much, at unexpected moments he could say something that would surprise you.

Eddie's sister Christine: "One of the guys [in the ski group] told a story: he said, 'we were in Spain, and we're going past this building and there was something written in Latin on it. Eddie stops, and tells me what it says.' "

Studying Latin was one of Eddie's more recent interests. A longstanding passion of his, however, was the study of geography and maps. He always seemed to understand how the terrain at ground level matched up with the big picture. From his seat in the back of the minivan, Eddie noticed that after crossing the Teton Pass the road leveled out, only to rise into the mountains again after crossing the state border from Idaho back into Wyoming.

Eddie had been to Jackson Hole once before on a trip with LISG founder Fred, and Fred's daughter, but he had never been to Targhee. He had taken this opportunity of re-visiting the Tetons to do some reading prior to the trip. He had discovered that the name "Teton" derives from the French fur-trappers and mountain men of the 19th Century who made a living from the plentiful animal life in the region. It was so named because of its three prominent peaks: *les trois tetons* (three breasts) known as Grand Teton, Middle Teton and South Teton. The fame of the Tetons stems from their lack of foothills, creating a dramatic rise of mountain to almost 7,000 feet above the valley floor.

Eddie had also read that the Tetons and Jackson Hole had been location shoots for several films and television shows, including John Wayne's acting debut in The Big Trail in 1930. *I've heard a lot about this place,* Eddie thought. *The powder at Targhee is supposed to be great. They're supposed to get 500 inches a year. I'm going to ski all day long. That breakfast from the Parkway Inn should hold me till dinnertime.*

Finally, the grand entrance to Grand Targhee loomed before them: a giant pi symbol made out of timber, topped by a sign reading 'Welcome to Grand Targhee,' with the supports flanked by smaller vertical posts that provide a warm and fuzzy feeling of symmetry. Entering the parking lot, the group could see immediately that Targhee was a much smaller operation than Jackson Hole. The parking lot, in fact, was about a fifth of the size of that of the average Long Island Walmart.

Targhee has only two mountains and three major lifts. An additional small lift is situated in the kids and beginners area. The base of the resort, immediately in front of the parking lot, features a wide set of stairs leading to a few shops and a couple of restaurants in the base village. If you lose track of your friends, you can meet up at the "tower," the major landmark, right next to the parking lot before one ascends the stairs.

When a New Yorker hears the word tower, he/she tends to look for something on the order of the Empire State Building.

The Targhee tower, by contrast, is only four stories tall. It houses the ski repair shop, the locker room, a counter where one can purchase photographs of oneself taken while hopefully executing a cool looking maneuver on one's skis or snowboard, a pool and spa, a restaurant, and the First Aid Room slash patrol room.

Once outside again, go up the stairs to find a general store (complete with whatever libations are most apropos—coffee, tea, beer, wine, etc.); an outdoor outfitters with clothing and other accoutrements, a snowboard shop, the ticket office, and a bar/restaurant called the Trap Bar—the resort's decompression chamber after a hard day on the slopes. And that's about it. A tiny base village, two mountains, three main lifts—it's hard to imagine someone could get lost here. Yet it happened, repeatedly—particularly along the resort's north boundary line.

When you work at a place for awhile, you tend to develop That's The Way We've Always Done Things Around Here Syndrome. Sometimes it takes a new person to notice that all is not well. Someone with good observational skills—someone like newbie ski patroller Mandy Jones. It was Mandy's first year working as a ski instructor and patroller at Targhee. She had grown up in the Finger Lake region of New York State and had started alpine (downhill) skiing at the age of three. At nine years old her interest in the sport intensified and she began to ski regularly. At sixteen she was hired as a professional certified ski instructor at Bristol Mountain in her home state. She was interested in working ski patrol and ski instruction at a small resort, so when her best friend invited her to come out to Idaho, Mandy took advantage of the opportunity and was hired at Grand Targhee as both a ski instructor and a patroller. Also an excellent photographer, she held a degree in Fine Arts from a Colorado university.

Photographers need to be keen observers, and Mandy was true to her calling. Even in the short time she'd been employed there, she had noticed some issues with the vagueness of the indicators of the resort's northern boundary.

Mandy Jones: "There is nothing continuous or clearly marked. There are sporadic pieces of bamboo. Some are just single sticks of bamboo that act as more of a reference point in the fog for the snowcats who are grooming so they don't go off that cat track. Then some of the bamboo have small circular signs that say 'closed' on them. And then very sporadically, maybe only two or three on that whole line of that north boundary, are two-by-two square orange posts that then have mounted on them rectangular 'closed' tags... It's very vaguely marked. And this is a location of concern because we had ... someone displaced in this area approximately four to six weeks prior to Ed's incident. A young boy was skiing with his brother and ended up out in the same area [as Eddie]. His only saving grace was he was there on a very clear day and his brother had the sense to come to ski patrol with a handset radio that they had been communicating on and say 'my brother is lost, can you talk him back in.' So we had experience that we had lost someone out there recently. It was obvious to us [Ski Patrol] it was vague to customers."

On the morning of January 19, 2010, while Mandy, Kris, Andrew, Jared, Bill and the other Targhee patrollers were doing their daily tasks of sweeps and checkpoints, the LISG buses were arriving in the parking lot. After picking up their lift tickets, some LISG folks went to the locker room to change while others headed straight to the base of the Dreamcatcher lift. Fred had instructed them to be back in time for a 4 p.m. departure.

Eddie was always anxious to ski, taking advantage of every possible moment. He was already at the top of the mountain when Cheryl, Rich, Ross and Marco got there at 10 a.m., wearing the outfit he always wore: red Coolar jacket, black pants, hat, black gloves, goggles.

Cheryl: "The group was lagging a little bit, so we were pretty much the first people on the lift from our group, and we got to the top of the mountain and Eddie was standing there by himself and so I asked Eddie, 'Do you have anyone to ski with?' He sort of indicated that he didn't, so I said, 'Well, then, why don't you ski with us?' And he just was like, 'Okay.' And he just tagged along."

At the top of Fred's Mountain, elevation 9,862 feet, on a bluebird day you can get some incredible photos of the area. To the south, Mt. Moran at 12,605 feet; to the west are Mount Owen at 12,928 feet and the three Tetons—Grand, Middle and South. Grand Teton tops out at 13,770 feet. But unfortunately on this day it was snowing, windy, and cloudy as the five of them convened at the summit, prompting Cheryl to complain to Rich, "Geez, I'm lugging this camera for nothing, you can't see a thing!"

"I know," said Rich. "Hey guys," he motioned to Marco, Ross and Eddie, "let's stick together, okay? Visibility is not that great." They all nodded and proceeded down the Crazy Horse trail near the top of the Dreamcatcher lift. Crazy Horse was blue-squared on the Targhee trail map, indicating 'Difficult.'

Cheryl used fat skis—Vocal Ridge 164's, while Eddie's skis were thinner, more suited to groomed trails. Ross, Marco and Rich were on snowboards. After skiing runs from the Dreamcatcher lift until 10:45 or so, the group headed for the trails off the Blackfoot lift. They went down Williamson Bowl which lands right at the bottom of the lift. They then went for the tops of Ravenwood and Lost Warrior, making their way toward skier's left to pick up the Williamson Bowl trail again. They rode Blackfoot back up and came down Steamvent to Funnel, an easier run. Around 11:30 a.m. they returned to the base of Dreamcatcher. It was still snowing, with another couple of inches having accumulated since the morning runs.

"I'm starving," Cheryl said. "Do you guys want to take a break?" Ross, Marco and Rich nodded in assent. They skied over to the racks and began taking off their gear.

"Where's Cola?" asked Marco. He looked to his right and spotted Eddie examining the large map posted at the base of the lift.

"Eddie, we are stopping to take a break," Cheryl called. Eddie looked at them and waved. He was going to continue skiing.

Cheryl: "He always seemed to know his way. We never had to worry about him being the last one off the mountain or anything. He was definitely a safe skier. Usually the slower of the group; [he] would make his turns very, like, precision. He was sort of a stiff skier, but he was never aggressive—by no means."

As they were leaving, Cheryl turned and saw Eddie making his way over toward the Dreamcatcher lift. This was the last time she ever saw him.

* * *

Larry woke up around 9:30 a.m. in his room on the second floor of the Parkway Inn. His roommate John was already gone, and so was most of the ski group. *I guess everyone's out on the mountain,* he thought. *I've practically got the whole place to myself.* Today was shopping day. The goal: a cool cowboy hat. Should be easy to find one in this town, where every single piece of decor was all about the Old West. Then there were gifts to bring home. He was sure there'd be no shortage of items to choose from.

He took a leisurely shower, shaved, dressed, and opened the curtains to check out the weather. It was cloudy and overcast, a few flakes were drifting by but it wasn't really snowing, at least not on this side of the Teton Pass. He was looking forward to strolling around the Jackson town square, only a few blocks walk from the Parkway. It looked like a good day for walking around. For himself, he hoped it wouldn't snow so he could explore the town more easily, but he knew as far as his ski buddies were concerned, the more snow the merrier. He needn't worry; he didn't know it, but the snowfall was already heavy over at Targhee, forty five miles to the north.

Larry grabbed his jacket and went downstairs. He suddenly remembered he had left his brown T shirt in the pool area, so instead of going to the lobby he took a left and went outside to the annex, where the pool and hot tubs are. Steam was coming off the top of the hot tubs; he made a mental note to hit that this afternoon. The shirt was still lying on the chair where he'd left it the night before. He retrieved it and went back up to his room and tossed it on the bed before going downstairs again. The lobby was empty, and one of the girls was working in the little office behind the front desk.

"Hi, how you doing?" he said to her as she looked up.

"Fine thank you. Can I help you with something?"

"Is there any coffee left?" Larry really needed some coffee right away.

"No," she laughed, "Your friends drank four thermoses full—but I can make some more."

"No it's okay," Larry said. He figured he could grab a cup from one of the cafes while he was walking around town. He put on his jacket and stepped out the front door. The streets were empty. It was now about 10:30 and apparently everyone in town was already where they needed to be. He made a left out the front door walked up Deloney a couple blocks, where he made a left onto North Glenwood. He spotted the Lotus Cafe—perfect for a morning coffee and muffin. He went in.

* * *

Ski resorts are quite keen on maintaining a good relationship with their local ski communities. Ninety percent of western ski resorts are on public lands, and resort policies regarding boundaries are often overlooked when it comes to the locals. The resort administration rationale being, "the locals know the area so we don't have to hold their hand."

Backcountry skiing is the fastest-growing segment of the industry, with skiers, snowboarders, climbers and snowmobilers continually searching for fresh descents.

Ski resorts do not cater only to alpine, or downhill, skiers. In recent years the art of snowboarding—essentially a wide ski, or skateboard without wheels— has entered the mainstream. Additionally, the sport of skiing includes a completely different approach known as Nordic, or Cross Country, skiing. Nordic skis are thinner than downhill skis, and the boot bindings clip to the skis only at the toe. This leaves the heel free to rise up off the ski when one is on flat terrain. Unlike Alpine skiing, Nordic skiing allows flat and uphill skiing in addition to downhill. As one can imagine, propelling one's skis on flats or uphill is quite a workout.

In both Alpine and Nordic skiing there are two basic divisions: trails, or backcountry. Ski trails offer a more controlled environment, especially when the trails are groomed— smoothed out by machines and/or previous skiers. Off-resort backcountry skiing, on the other hand, gives the skier a sense of exploring new territory in a more solitary environment; the skier must usually make his/her own trail in unmarked snow ("off-piste"), which is an attraction for those with more advanced skills. Plus, it's free—if you are skiing elsewhere than at a resort. Backcountry alpine skiers carry "skins" in their pack; these are thin layers made of nylon or mohair that clip onto the tips and tails of the skis and provide the traction necessary for the skier to re-ascend the mountain, since there are no ski lifts in the backcountry.

Even inside the resort there are inherent dangers in the sport of skiing. The most obvious is the possibility of injury due to falling, or hitting a tree or other obstacle. Frostbite is also a concern.

Eddie's sister Christine: "I have two toes on my right foot that got frostbite, and now every winter they always get numb. At Mont Tremblant in 1980 we all got frostbite. It was the coldest winter they ever had. It didn't stop us, we still skied."

The most dramatic danger on the slopes is the threat of avalanche. Obviously ski resorts and mountains go hand in hand, so one of the functions of a resort's ski patrol team is mitigating avalanche risk. Before 1980 there were rarely more than 10 avalanche deaths in the United States in the winter. There are now more than 30. (The figure is gradually increasing due to the prevalence of "extreme" sports that push the envelope, as well as global climate change.) An avalanche occurs without warning, and those caught in its path will likely find themselves buried under a mass of snow that hardens instantly to a cement-like consistency. A frequent cause of death for an avalanche victim is suffocation. For this reason, backcountry skiers will always carry a pack that includes a portable shovel, collapsible probe, and beacon. The beacon can be set to either send or receive a signal. In the aftermath of an avalanche, unless a ski or a body part is sticking up out of the snow, rescuers have no way of visually locating victims who may have been swept over large distances. By setting their beacons to receive, rescue teams are able to locate beacons that were set to transmit, worn by skiers buried beneath feet of snow.

The " Skier Responsibility Code," a code of ethics for those enjoying winter mountain activities, was established by the National Ski Areas Association in 1966. The reverse side of a Grand Targhee lift ticket contains a synopsis of this code, along with mention of the Inherent Risk policy (needless to say, to fit all this on the back of a lift ticket requires very small print):

Acknowledgement and Acceptance of Risks and Liability Release
Please Read Carefully!

All forms of skiing, snowboarding, and any other activities at Grand Targhee Resort are inherently hazardous and require the deliberate and conscious control of your physical body through the proper use of equipment in relation to ever-changing variables and dangers. Safety is directly affected by your judgement in the severe elements of high mountain forest terrain.

Ski or ride only within your own ability. Be alert to continually changing weather, visibility and surface conditions; surface or sub-surface snow or ice; cliffs rocks; ruts; stumps; trees; streams; avalanches closed areas; natural and man-made objects and features which may or may not be marked; grooming and snowmaking activities and equipment; snowmobiles; lift, mechanical and equipment failures; and collisions with others. Falls and injuries occur and are a common occurrence while participating in these activities.

I acknowledge and accept all of the RISKS of skiing, snowboarding and other activities at Grand Targhee Resort. I AGREE NOT TO BRING A CLAIM AGAINST NOR SUE GRAND TARGHEE RESORT, LLC, its parent companies, subsidiaries, affiliates, owners, officers, directors agents, employees, sponsors, insurance carriers and landowner (hereinafter RELEASEES) for any and all INJURY or DAMAGE that may result from the inherent risks and dangers of participating in any activities at Grand Targhee.

As a condition of being permitted to use the resort area, lifts and trails, I agree to SAVE AND HOLD HARMLESS, RELEASE AND INDEMNIFY RELEASEES from any and all liability for personal injury, death or property damage resulting in any way from my participation in skiing, snowboarding, the use of lifts or other equipment, the condition of the premises, and including any and all liability that may result from RELEASEES acts of negligence, or any other person or cause. I further agree that any claim that I may bring at anytime for any reason against

Grand Targhee Resort shall be submitted to the jurisdiction of the State Court in Teton County, Wyoming, and shall be governed by the laws of Wyoming. If any portion of this agreement is deemed unenforceable, all other parts shall remain in full force and effect.

No Refunds - Not Transferable

Patroller Mandy Jones snowplowed as she approached the base of the Sacajawea lift tower on her morning sweep. She came to a full stop and reached out a gloved hand to the rip in the tower padding. A spray of snow from the rear startled her, and she turned to see Jared grinning as he lifted a ski pole in greeting.

"Are you done with your sweep already?" she asked.

"Yep. I thought I would see if you needed any help."

Mandy frowned. "I'm just looking at this tear. It seems like it will hold for awhile if no one hits the padding. Does that happen a lot at this tower?"

"Not really. But it could, I guess. Hey Mandy ..."

"Yes Jared?"

"Do you ... I mean, would you, uh, want to catch a movie later or something?"

Mandy hesitated. She didn't want to hurt his feelings. "I'm sorry Jared, I have to work on my photography portfolio tonight. But I'll probably see you at the Common House if you go for dinner."

"Okay. Later." He skied off quickly.

He's so cute, she thought. *But remember Rule Number One—Don't get involved with someone you work with!* She glared at the rip in the tower pad once more. There wasn't any metal showing. It certainly looked like it could withstand at least one more skier slamming into it by accident.

* * *

Before the days of high-tech leg-stabilizing orthopedic devices, high school students in more affluent communities could count upon at least on classmate a year returning from Christmas vacation sporting a leg in a cast. (The hunt would then be on for magic markers, because all of the classmate's friends would have to sign the cast and ball point pen didn't work so well on plaster.) The injured party's parents were not able to sue the ski resort because of the "Inherent Risk" policy.

A ski resort will cry "Inherent Risk" at the merest suggestion of a lawsuit. The Inherent Risk policy was enacted by providers of outdoor activities to curb frivolous lawsuits and to protect their businesses. Naturally, disputes arise when these outdoor-recreation providers downplay the risks involved in the activities they offer, or use the Inherent Risk policy to justify laxity in standard safety measures.

The WyoFile website, a division of Wyoming Public Media, notes in a 2011 article: *The Wyoming Recreation Safety Act makes clear that clients of recreation companies assume the "inherent risk" of the activity in which they're participating. The law has been described as the one of the strongest in the country at providing protections for outdoor-recreation companies, and lawmakers have bolstered it more than once. Courts have not only thrown out lawsuits in clear-cut cases—like the skier who died after willingly going off a 25-foot terrain-park jump at Jackson Hole—but have also rejected claims in less-obvious cases, including injuries resulting from slipping saddles and chair lifts... "Consumers in Wyoming are now faced with an entire industry whose economic and consequent legislative power enables them to conduct business with only a passing thought to the safety of those who utilize their services," William F. Downes, a federal district-court judge, editorialized back in 1998, in his opinion that dismissed the claim brought by a man who was injured when his saddle slipped.*

In any sport, when play goes out of bounds everything stops. When skiers and snowboarders intentionally go out of bounds, the resort stops being responsible for their safety. This is clearly stated in the Skiers Responsibility Code—but the key word is "intentionally." What guidelines apply when the skier UN-intentionally goes out of bounds? This is a grey area because the determination of intentionality depends upon the circumstances.

In what's known as a "soft closure," the ski industry standard issue 'closed' signs are typically posted at regular intervals along boundary lines. At Grand Targhee these are 9-inch by 13-inch yellow plastic signs mounted on bamboo poles. A "hard closure," by contrast, refers to a boundary marked by a rope. Even so, rope-ducking happens often. In the quest for powder snow, the more adventurous—or foolhardy—often will have no qualms about ducking the rope to get to it. Once someone ducks a rope, he/she has violated the Skier Responsibility Code. Trying to sue the resort after getting hurt while inbounds is hard enough, so if you were out of bounds, as they say in New York, fuhgeddaboudit.

Ski areas in the western United States are particularly vulnerable to having skiers get lost after intentionally or unintentionally going outside of the ski area's boundaries. Just like neighboring ski areas of Jackson Hole, Sun Valley and Big Sky, Grand Targhee has had a number of out-of-area searches in its history. Once incident occurred on Feb. 14, 2001 when 20-year-old Colin O'Farrell ducked a rope, "poaching powder and traversing back in so I could pick up the cat track... one run I got below my traverse... one bad decision after another." He ended up in South Leigh Canyon where he inadvertently slipped into the creek at one point and got wet. He dug a snow cave and spent the night there after the ski patrol's unsuccessful search. He was found by helicopter the next morning and taken to the hospital where he was treated for frostbite.

Another incident occurred on Feb. 4, 2006, when a 911 call came in at 2:30 p.m. from a lost skier who had "taken a right off of the main lift and was in dense trees." The ski patrol found a track leaving the North Boundary Traverse cat road, followed it down into South Leigh Canyon, and found the skier more than three hours later at 5:45 p.m. More recent incidents had occurred as well, such as the one Mandy Jones reported involving two brothers, the younger of whom had to be talked back into the resort via radio communication.

Skiers and snowboarders are highly aware that they are engaged in a sport that not everyone can do. It's physical, it requires a high degree of coordination and practice, and it requires money. Even the most mild-mannered among them can tend toward a little showing off at times, so it's no surprise that ski patrollers and Search and Rescue personnel often find themselves having to deal with people who have disregarded the rules in one way or another.

In the aftermath of Eddie "Cola's" death, Eddie's father got ahold of Don Oscar, the Commander of Teton County Wyoming Search and Rescue, on the telephone. Oscar told him that Eddie had ducked a rope. Ed Fitzgerald Sr. was an avid skier himself—he knew what that meant. It meant 'Case Closed.'

Ed Sr.. hadn't skied with Eddie for years; he knew he hadn't taught his son to duck ropes, but perhaps Eddie had picked up some bad habits over time. Ed hadn't been there with Eddie, and he didn't know the area. If Don Oscar said that Eddie had ducked a rope, how was Ed to have disputed it? It wasn't until Eddie's memorial service that another picture began to emerge—one that contradicted everything Don Oscar had said.

Chapter 3
The Afternoon Of January 19

"They knew the guy was from New York and didn't have any backcountry skills...I don't know why they called off that search. It was a little bit stormy...but there's only one canyon he could have been in. So everybody knew where he was."
—ER nurse Gabe Mender

Eddie Cola waved goodbye to Cheryl, Rich, Marco and Ross as they prepared to break for lunch. They went into the lodge and Eddie got back onto the Dreamcatcher lift and rode up to the top of Fred's Mountain again. He was skiing by himself now. He had done many of the blue square trails earlier in the day with the group, and was now looking for the black diamonds, the 'expert' trails. This time he went to skier's left, skiing down through Happy Hunting Ground to the black diamond trail section. *I didn't come all the way to Wyoming to waste time eating. It's a little hard to see but I don't know when I'll ever be back here so I'm going to ski till the bus leaves.*

Eddie felt like a tiny figure inside a giant snow globe, it was so foggy at the top of the mountain and he was skiing through so much powder. He was aware there were other people on the mountain, he could hear them. Someone was actually yodeling. That was a blessing because he was being very careful not to run into anyone and it always helped when people were making noise. Continually skiing down Fred's Mountain and then taking Dreamcatcher back up, he encountered easier terrain, much like what he had skied earlier with the group. Nice, easy. But he wanted to tackle a few more black diamonds. Even though on a foggy, snowy day like today, most skiers had chosen the blue square runs instead of black diamond runs.

When Eddie was skiing, he felt more alive and more happy than at any other time. He lived to ski. During spring, summer and autumn he rode his bike to stay in shape for winter skiing; and of course his daily postal delivery route had him walking seven or eight miles a day all year 'round.

All his life the thing Eddie wanted most was to be normal. His entire childhood was spent going to doctors and attending special schools. But he was not unintelligent. In fact, he was smarter than most people. Because he rarely spoke, however, even those closest to him didn't always know it.

Christine, Eddie's sister: "Eddie was a savant. I found that out when I typed one of his college papers. I was blown away. I had no idea how smart he was until then."

People who were his intellectual equals avoided Eddie. When he was a kid the other kids made fun of him because he couldn't talk very well. He couldn't write very well either. He was skinny back then, and that never changed. He could eat anything and not gain weight. And he wasn't, to put it mildly, the most coordinated person. He couldn't dance. As a kid, it had taken him the better part of a year to learn how to ride a two-wheeler without training wheels. In his neighborhood of Forest Hills, crossing Queens Boulevard was like an Olympic event—he had to gear up for it, prepare physically and mentally in order to cross six lanes of New York traffic.

Ed Fitzgerald Sr.: "When [Eddie] was young, he went fishing with his uncle in New Jersey and fell off the dock, prompting his uncle to jump in the water and save him. [His mother and I] determined both he and Christine had to learn to swim. We took him to the Forest Hills

Community House where he and Christine learned to swim and to race. Eddie was bullied by the kids in the locker room and consequently neither he nor Christine participated in other activities, even though the Community House was the center of young people's activities in Forest Hills Gardens. I am reminded of an incident early in his life (perhaps 3 or 4 years old) when we went to Wellesley for Christmas at my parents' house. I had bought a football, helmet and shoulder pads and Eddie was sitting on the floor by the Christmas tree surrounded by these and many other toys. My father commented that it reminded him of Ferdinand the Bull. (I am sure you know the story of Ferdinand sitting among the flowers in typical un-bull-like fashion.)"

When Eddie was hired at the Post Office and met his buddy Fred McKuen, he got back into the sport he hadn't had time for while he was in college. Eddie began to ski every chance he could get, as if to make up for lost time. Skiing every weekend, skiing during his annual vacation from work, thinking skiing, breathing skiing. When he was on skis, he was normal. Just like other folks. Better, even, because skiing well was a real skill.

Eddie thought it was odd not to come across anyone else from the Long Island Ski Group, but he wasn't going to let that stop him—he continued to ski by himself. After a few more runs he paused at the base of the Dreamcatcher lift to enjoy the moment. It was around 1 p.m. and it was still snowing heavily. He was on his skis, in his element. The rear of the base village was right in front of him, and he watched people go by for a few moments.

It was surprising how few people were on the slopes, given the excellent snow. He still didn't see anybody else from the ski group. *Is it possible every single one of them is already at the bar, with three more good hours of skiing left before the bus leaves?* Okay, visibility wasn't great and it was snowing, but hey—this was the only chance to take advantage of the famous Targhee experience on this trip. He was starting to feel a little bit hungry though. *Maybe I should get a Power Bar or something.* He contemplated taking off his skis and racking them for ten minutes, long enough to clump down the steps in his ski boots and go into that Trading Post shop, but ... *hell with it.* He loaded onto Dreamcatcher, once again all by himself on the quad lift—just like Targhee advertises: "you can ride the lift alone." On the way up he scanned the mountain for any familiar jackets. But it was snowing and difficult to see.

At the summit once more, he found himself in near white-out conditions. He decided to return to the Blackfoot lift where he had skied earlier with the group. Because Rich, Marco and Ross had been on snowboards, even less-suited for flatter terrain than skies, the group had stayed near the summit and not gone all the way down. This time Eddie took the Headwall Traverse to get from the top of Dreamcatcher to the top of Blackfoot. The Blackfoot lift was only a two-seater, as opposed to the others that were newer quad lifts. This section of the resort, however, had the most open-looking trails.

There was a map posted at the top of the Blackfoot lift. It showed a large area to skier's right completely open for skiing. No boundary was indicated; it looked to Eddie as if he could ski all the way down from here, and come out by the kid's area. *Okay, last few runs of the day. This is gonna be fun.*

* * *

"Complain, complain, complain," said Ross.

"C'mon," responded Cheryl defensively, "don't your legs hurt too, after yesterday at Jackson Hole?"

"Yeah, a little, but so what?"

Rich put his hand on his wife's shoulder. "That's part of skiing, honey."

"I know it's part of skiing, duh! I just said my legs hurt, that's all. Why are you guys getting on my case?"

"Now, now, children," said Marco. "Don't fight."

"Who gets the roast beef," said the female server, approaching with a platter with four sandwiches.

"Right here, thanks," Ross said.

She passed around the other plates, her memory of everyone's order evidently restored, although it probably helped that everyone else had ordered the chicken sandwich. The guys tore into the sandwiches as Cheryl reached into a small plastic bag from the Trading Post.

"What'd you buy?" asked Rich between bites.

"Advil. Christ, my legs are really killing me."

Marco reached for the salt shaker and said, "You going back out?"

"Oh yeah, of course," Cheryl replied. "I'm going back out definitely, but I don't know how much longer I can last."

"The snow is really good here but the weather kind of sucks," Marco commented.

"Doesn't suck enough for Eddie Cola," Ross said. "He's still out there."

Marco said "Don't be surprised to see Cola walking in here any minute, you know his appetite."

They finished their meals and Rich said, "Well, everyone ready for another run? I'm just gonna hit the head. See you out there."

After bathroom breaks and locker room visitations the group reconvened at the ski racks. "Wanna do that Sacajawea chair now, check out the other mountain?" asked Cheryl of the guys.

"Oh, so now you're fully recovered?" asked Ross. Cheryl took off her glove and hit him with it.

"Let's go back up Dreamcatcher and snowboard around there some more, then we can make our way over to that other chair," Rich said. A nodding of heads all around indicated the plan was a good one.

* * *

"C'mon Mario, let's do one more run," Freddie cajoled him. "You're doing great for an *old* guy."   Fred McKuen's nephew Freddie was a forty year old man, but he was still a generation behind Mario and he enjoyed teasing him. They had only met for the first time at the beginning of this trip, but had taken a liking to each other right away. "I'm a little nervous," Freddie had told Mario. "I haven't skied in a long time."

"You found the right guy," Mario had replied. "Because I don't go where everybody else goes. If I see moguls, I don't go that way."

Mario had been skiing with the LISG since the 1980's. He had been on most of the trips. Even a prior skiing accident resulting in not one, but two, broken legs had not stopped him from pursuing the sport.

"Ready, old man?" asked Freddie again.

"Hey Junior, watch it now," said Mario. "Respect your elders why don't ya?" He raised his goggles and gave Freddie an exaggerated glare. Freddie laughed. He was making fun of his new friend, but he secretly hoped that in twenty years he himself would look as fit as Mario did. At 5-foot seven inches and 138 pounds, Mario was in excellent shape, unlike many of his friends he'd grown up with who didn't exercise. They'd let themselves go and had the aches and pains to prove it.

Mario stretched his back out, then kicked the ski rack gently, with the edge of his ski, to knock some stubborn snow out of the binding. He had given the younger man some tips on how to make his turns smoother, and Freddie had already shown improvement. Mario was nearly ready to call it a day, what with the crappy visibility and all, but the "kid" wanted one more run, hell. "Okay, let's do it," Mario agreed.

He and Freddie loaded back onto the lift. "Have you seen Eddie?" asked Mario as they rode up the mountain. Mario and Eddie were best friends, though their differing skiing levels usually had them separated on the slopes.

"Nope," Freddie replied.

"Wasn't that him like, half an hour ago, down near that traverse near the base?"

"Don't know. I didn't see him," said Freddie.

"Well," Mario said, laughing, "I know he's havin' a ball, wherever he is." At the summit, Mario and Freddie got off the lift and looked around, trying to soak in the majesty of the area's famous scenic peaks—difficult, through the snow and fog. Mario reached inside his jacket to zip his fleece layer all the way up. The wind was strong and a few big flakes had already gone where they weren't welcome.

Freddie crouched down to pull up his socks. Mario spit into his goggles and rubbed the saliva on the inside of the lenses—that usually helped stop them from fogging up. There was already enough fog outside, he didn't need any more inside his goggles. He shaded his eyes and tried to see through the misty veil that shrouded their surroundings. The falling snow suddenly reminded him of his youth in Long Island, when winters had record snowfalls quite often. That was no longer the case, but he didn't know why. Some people he knew said it was because of global warming, but Mario wasn't sure. All he knew right then was that he could hardly see a few feet in front of him, and the last thing he wanted was to have a head-on collision with a tree.

"You know what I heard?" he said to Freddie.

"What?"

"They have a nickname for this place. It's called Grand Targhee, right? So they call it "Grand Fogg-ie.""

Freddie laughed. "That's a good one. Good name, definitely. You can't see shit."

Mario turned to Freddie and looked him straight in the eye. "Hey, kid, this is the last run for me, just so's ya know. I'm gonna be done after this."

"Okay, no problem." Freddie patted him on the back and yelled "YeeeeeHAAAAA!" as they pushed off and proceeded down the mountain into the misty whiteness. Mario had been next to him but not two minutes into the run, Freddie could no longer see him. He wanted to enjoy himself, but the disconcerting feeling of not being able to see more than ten feet or so ahead gnawed at his pleasure.

Freddie cut to the right, then the left, arcing so he had more time to see what lay ahead of him. Powder flew up around him. He felt like he was in a scene in one of those ski movies. *This is so classic.* He slowed down, his goggles were slipping a little over his knit cap. His pole dangled in the air for a few seconds as he adjusted them with his right hand. *There, that's better. Now to catch up with Mario. Where IS that old man? No prob, we'll meet up at the base.* But in another minute he was jolted from his focus when a blood-curdling scream pierced the thick air. Freddie snowplowed and turned his head, searching for the source. Somebody must be hurt, bad!

The scream happened again, along with a choice selection of New York's best expletives. It was coming from up ahead of him. *Shit, it's Mario!* Freddie skied down the slope and found Mario lying in the snow, his left ski boot grotesquely twisted around so that it was facing backward. He was groaning and pounding his fist on the snow.

"Mario, hold on, I'll get help, hold on!" Freddie yelled. He shaded his eyes and looked up toward the summit. There didn't seem to be anyone around. He wondered if he should ski down to try and get help, or wait with Mario? *Someone has to come along, please!* Suddenly, as if in answer to his prayers, two women skiers in red ski patrol jackets came into view on their way down the mountain.

"Help, please, stop, help!" cried Freddie. "My friend is hurt, can you get help!" The women skied over.

"Oh my God," said the one in the pink hat, softly. She knelt down next to Mario who was writhing in the snow, his face pale and contorted.

"I'll radio for assistance, don't worry," said the other one with the red hat. She took a hand-held radio out of her day pack and called patrol dispatch. Hearing the official-sounding radio static was somehow comforting to Freddie. He knelt in the snow next to Mario. The pink hatted woman cradled Mario's head in her gloved hands. Freddie gripped Mario's shoulder. "OK, they're on the way, hang on. We're gonna get you to the hospital, don't worry."

Freddie had never seen anyone with this horrific an injury. *Jesus, his foot is totally turned around!* But he couldn't allow himself to be freaked out. He had to be there for Mario. *Just keep talking to him. If that was me, I'd want someone to be there for me, talk to me.* Freddie reached over to take Mario's ski pole out of his glove.

"Don't move him!" said the ski patrol woman forcefully.

"No, I'm not," Freddie said. "I'm just getting his ski pole out."

"Okay," said the other one. "They should be here in a minute. Hang on sir. Try to be still." She looked at Freddie. "What's his name?"

"Mario."

"Hang on Mario," the ski patrol woman said, then she got back on the radio to give landmarks to the dispatcher. Mario turned his head back and forth. He brought his gloved hand to his face and pushed up his goggles.

In exactly six minutes, two more patrollers arrived, a male and a female, with a rescue toboggan. "What's his name?" said the newly-arrived female patroller to Freddie.

"Mario."

"OK Mario, hold on, we're going to put a splint on you. What happened to you?"

"I couldn't see, I couldn't see!" Mario whined. "I hit a rock or something, I just went over, like a somersault ..."

"Happens to the best of us," said the male patroller. He and his companion kneeled beside Mario and tended to his injury. It took about fifteen minutes to apply the temporary splint to stabilize Mario's leg and carefully ease him onto the toboggan.

The male ski patroller spoke in a comforting tone, "Now Mario, we're going to lift you onto the sled, and get you down to the First Aid Room, then they'll get you to the hospital. OK?"

"Yeah."

"Where's the First Aid Room?" Freddie asked.

"It's downstairs in the tower building, make a left, it's near the end of the hall," said the male patroller. He and the other patroller who had responded began to make their way down the mountain with Mario strapped to the rescue toboggan.

"I'm right behind you Mario!" Freddie called after them. Left alone with the first ski patrol women, he said, "Wow, it's so lucky you came by when you did, thanks a lot!"

"No problem, I hope your friend is okay," said the one in the pink hat. "Looks pretty bad though," she added.

"I never saw a leg broken like that," said Freddie. "But you must've seen lots of bad injuries, being on the ski patrol."

"Actually I'm just a volunteer, I'm not a regular ski patrol member," she said. "But yeah, I'm glad I could help out."

"The ambulance will come right to the back door of the First Aid Room," said the other one in the red hat. "Then they'll just wheel him right out to it."

"Do you think I can ride in the ambulance with him?" Freddie asked.

"Yeah, I don't think that will be a problem."

"Okay, that's good. Listen, um, thanks again ladies, I don't know what I would've done if you hadn't come by," said Freddie, extending his gloved hand.

"Don't worry about it," said the volunteer patroller. "Hey, listen, we have to keep going. You should go on down to the First Aid Room to be with your friend." She reminded him of the location, and he nodded. He sighed as he watched the two women ski down the mountain. *Poor Mario. Shit.*

* * *

"Hey guys, I'm done," said Cheryl at about 1:30 p.m. She was not comfortable on her skis at all, feeling the ice underneath the powder. It made for a rather unstable sensation. That, plus the crappy weather, and her legs being sore, was a recipe that called for an immediate glass of wine, if not two glasses.

Rich, Marco and Ross accompanied her back to the base where they ran into Ted Knowlton, the fireman—another Long Island Ski Group regular. Ted was scrutinizing the map posted next to the lift. He saw them and raised his glove in greeting. Rich glided over on his board. "Hey Ted, what's up."

"Not much. Nice snow huh?"

"Yeah. You going up again?"

"Definitely. Hey did you hear about Mario?"

"What about Mario?"

"He broke his leg. It's a bad break apparently."

"No! Didn't he already break his leg, once before?" Rich asked.

"He broke both his legs before," said Ted. "I forget what year it was."

"Geez, thanks for telling me. Wow. I guess he went to the hospital already?"

"Yeah, I think so."

"Okay. Hey, um, I'll see you on the bus."

Ted nodded. Rich unclipped his board and went over to where Cheryl was taking off her skis.

"Honey. Bad news."

* * *

Fred made a point of skiing with the new people.   On this trip there were quite a few. Fred had been skiing with all of them, and making friends, because word of mouth is the best kind of advertising. The more people signed up for the Long Island Ski Group trips, the better rate he could get from the tour operator.

Fred was careful to never have people make out checks to him or even to the group—they made them out directly to the tour operator. He didn't want to have to explain to the IRS why all that money was in his account one day and gone the next. Fred's cousin was an accountant and had explained to him how to handle the finances.

He tried to set up every detail of the trip in advance. Of course, there were always little glitches that you couldn't plan for—but Fred wanted to enjoy himself on the trip and not have to deal with last minute adjustments. He didn't like surprises.

He tried to ski with a different group every day. It was only around 12:30 and he'd already skied with two different parties; one group was a husband, wife and the wife's sister, from Pennsylvania. The other was a new guy named Jeff who owned a business right down the street from Fred's house in Glen Cove. With the Pennsylvania folks he had skied off both Sacajawea and Dreamcatcher in the morning. By the afternoon it was snowing pretty hard. He and Jeff had been at the top of Dreamcatcher and the lift operator said, "Why don't you go over to Blackfoot, there's a lot of snow there." That sounded good to Fred and Jeff, so they did.

The two men adjusted their gear and got ready to ski down what looked like some beautiful off-piste powder skiing between light trees. "Hey Jeff, I don't want to end up in a flat and have to hike back. Better stick close to the chair so we don't end up walking."

"Sounds good," Jeff replied. "Can you see okay Fred?"

"Yeah, yeah, I can see. I guess. But I'm going in after this run, okay?"

"Sure, no problem."

They skied down the blue trail Floyd's Fantasy, picking up the tail of Williamson Bowl toward the end. Jeff looked at Fred. "Hey, want to do one more before we call it quits? We can take that Steam—whatchamacallit, and cut through the kid's area to get back to base." Fred agreed and they did one more ride up Blackfoot, coming down Steamvent and Funnel. He was enjoying the powder but wasn't thrilled with the poor visibility. He looked at his watch and saw it was just before 1 p.m. "Lunchtime," he said when they got to the ski racks.

"Yup." They stomped the powder off their skis and headed for the locker room, where they changed into regular shoes. Jeff put on a fresh T shirt he'd brought with him.

"Jeff, I need to go to the cash machine, I'll catch you later," said Fred. He took his skis and boot bag and headed down the steps to the building where he'd seen the ATM earlier in the day, refreshed his wallet, and continued to the lodge. At the entrance he ran into a woman he knew was with the group from Florida, but didn't know anything else about her. She bore a resemblance to a girl he'd been in love with in high school.

"Hey, how are you," said Fred.

"Oh, just wonderful!" said the woman enthusiastically. She brushed back her shoulder-length blond hair and smiled. She was wearing jeans, sneakers, and a light colored sweater with sequins.

"You look like you're finished skiing for the day," Fred commented.

"Oh I don't ski. My husband does. You remember him, he's very tall, dark hair? He's the one with the loud lime green ski parka." She laughed. "We're friends of Nathan, that's how we found out about the trip."

Fred nodded and took a step backward. "Well, how are *you* doing, with him out there skiing?"

"Oh, I'm enjoying the trip," she replied. "The bus ride here today was wonderful, looking out the window. That mountain pass is incredible!"

"Yeah, it is," Fred agreed. "Great, I'm glad you're having a good time." His stomach was growling, he hoped she wouldn't notice. "Well, let me get some lunch here, I'm starving. Your husband knows the bus leaves at 4, right?"

"Oh yes, he knows. He's having a great time too, it looks like everyone is. But it's a shame about that man who broke his leg."

"What? Who broke his leg?" exclaimed Fred.

"I don't know his name. He was on the bus with us. Apparently he broke his leg pretty badly. Everyone's been talking about him. You mean you don't know about it?"

"Jesus!" Fred said, his chest tightening. *Who broke their leg? I gotta get to the ski patrol room and find out, they'll know. Christ!* He said goodbye to the Florida woman and asked a maintenance guy where the patrol room was. He was directed to the tower building and he rushed over there as fast as he could with his skis, his appetite having left him rather suddenly. He saw the counter where they sold photos and queried the girl there, who pointed to the hallway on her left. He ran up the ramp and knocked hard on the door that said "Ski Patrol—First Aid Room". A red-jacketed young man with a mountain man beard opened the door, and Fred's heart sank when he saw Mario lying on the bed on the left, with his nephew Freddie standing beside him. "That's my friend," said Fred, "he's in my tour group," and the patroller stood aside to let him in.

He rushed to Mario's bedside, joining his nephew Freddie. "Mario! What happened!"

"Shit Fred, I hit a rock, I tumbled head over heels. I couldn't see, man! I couldn't see a thing out there!"

Fred looked down at Mario's pale face, trying not to wince. "I know, I know, visibility was terrible, that's why I came in," he said. "What's going on? Are they taking you to the hospital?"

"Yeah," said Freddie, "the ambulance is on the way right now. He's got, like, a temporary splint on his leg. I'm gonna go to the hospital with him."

"Jesus, Mario, I'm so sorry!" Fred said, reaching over to squeeze his shoulder.

"Thank God Freddie here was with me," said Mario. Freddie, sitting in a chair next to the bed, patted Mario's good leg.

"Where were you?" asked Fred.

"I forget the name of the run. No, wait, it was Crazy Horse I think."

"Then what happened, you yelled for help?"

"At first there wasn't anyone there to call for help," Freddie told his uncle. "Then, it was like a miracle, these two girls showed up and one of 'em was a patroller so she called down to the ski patrol on her radio. Then they came and put him on a sled. On the way down I ran into some of our people, so they know about it."

Mario looked up at Fred. "Remember the last time, when I broke both my legs before?"

Fred nodded.

"This is worse, my friend. Much worse."

Fred waited with Mario and Freddie for the ambulance to arrive. It pulled up to the rear door of the First Aid Room and two paramedics wheeled in a gurney for Mario. The attending doctor, a young woman, had already turned Mario's foot back around while he screamed, applied an ice pack to the ankle, and replaced the splint that the patrollers had put on him to get him down to the base.

The paramedics carefully loaded Mario into the vehicle. Freddie squeezed in the back and sat next to his injured friend. His uncle Fred leaned in, putting his hand on Mario's good right leg as he lay on the gurney. "Hey, they're gonna take good care of you Mario. Don't worry. We'll come pick you up and you can ride back to the hotel with us on the bus."

Mario raised his hand to acknowledge he'd heard. He was in pain, but also slightly in shock. He closed his eyes tightly and gritted his teeth. The pain was bad, even with the meds he'd been given, but he knew it would get much worse as the night wore on. And so would his stress level. He was 61 years old. He had no medical insurance. *Why did I make that last run? I'm such an idiot! What was I trying to prove, that I could keep up with Freddie? Jesus Christ, I can't afford this, not again. Jesus Christ!*

One of the paramedics came around to the back and secured the door. "Don't worry, they'll get him fixed up in Driggs," he said to Fred.

"Thanks a lot, thanks," said Fred. He waited until the ambulance circled around with its lights flashing and drove toward the exit, then he returned to the First Aid Room to get Mario's and Freddie's equipment that they'd rented in Teton Village, propped up in the corner by the bed. He looked around for his own skis, which he was sure he'd left over by the back door. *Where are they? Shit, I left 'em right here! Jesus, would somebody take my skis? Christ, that's all I need, the fucking trip is ruined, Mario is fucked, and now somebody took my damn skis!*

"Are you looking for these?" asked one of the red-jacketed female patrollers, handing Fred his gear bag with his skis and poles.

"Yeah! Thanks! I left 'em right over there," he said, pointing to the corner of the room by the bed, "and then they weren't there."

"We just moved them so we could get him out. Don't worry, your friend will have a rough night, but they'll fix him up down in Driggs."

"Okay, thanks, thanks a lot. I better go tell the rest of my group."

Fred took his gear and left the tower building, going up the stairs to the bar. He expected that most of the group would be there. They all must know the bad news about Mario by now. Sure enough, when he walked in at least ten people rushed over to him.

"Fred! How is Mario? What's gonna happen to him now?"

"Is he in a lot of pain?"

"How is Mario getting back to New York then, can he still travel with us?"

"Did he already go to the hospital?"

"Does he have health insurance?"

Fred stood there hugging his skis with his left hand; he covered his face with his right arm. He felt like he was going to cry. This was the worst thing that had ever happened on one of his trips. "Geez, people, I don't know," he said in a muffled tone.

"Leave him alone," said Ted to the other skiers gathered around, "How should he know? We just have to wait and see what the doctor says."

"Where's Freddie," said Marco, ignoring Ted's directive. "Is he with Mario?"

"Mario already broke his leg once before," commented Cheryl.

"He broke both his legs before," said Ross, "He told me that yesterday on the bus."

"Jesus people!" said Ted, raising his voice.

"Fred, you saw him? How did he look?" asked Cheryl.

Fred wasn't in the mood to answer questions. "I need to think about this," he said, his voice barely audible. "I need a drink." He propped his skis up against the wall with the other LISG gear. Kathryn pointed him toward an empty bar stool and he ordered a Johnny Walker Black straight up, water on the side. Everyone was still crowding around him, asking more questions he couldn't answer. *Where's that drink? Christ!*

* * *

Why is the mountain so empty? Eddie wondered. He was at the summit, looking around for Long Island Ski Group people, particularly Mario. *Hey, maybe I can find Mario and ski with him before we go back to the bus.* He took out his cell phone. The battery was pretty low but he still had some juice left. The time was 2:13. He dialed Mario's cell and it went to voicemail. *Shit. Okay, I guess I'll just keep skiing by myself. I'll see him on the bus.*

* * *

Jon Alexander unzipped his red ski patrol jacket as he walked into the tower building. He was hungry, but because he had to fix that scheduling snafu with the cat-ski operators, and complete a sweep from one side of the mountain to the other, he hadn't had any time to eat. He still had to check in at the Patrol Room, and now lunch seemed even more unlikely.

In addition to his regular sweeps, as Assistant Director it was Jon's responsibility to keep tabs on all the patrollers, who did different sweeps each day. Rotating the sweeps was a good way to know the condition of all the runs, and ascertain what maintenance was needed in terms of rope lines, mountain signs and trail signs.

Jon liked being Director of Ski Patrol. Granted, it was only until his boss Pete Kerry returned, but as Assistant Director he was working his way up the ladder. He was getting a little too old for a $15 an hour job; the $900/week Director's salary is what he had his sights on. He knew that Pete was looking for another job, and after Pete left Targhee, Jon would naturally be promoted to Director.

Jon hoped he might have time to grab a sandwich before the meeting at 3:30. This was a daily meeting between the Director of Ski Patrol, the Marketing Manager, the Mountain Manager, the groomers and the Ski School director. During this meeting they would decide which runs would be groomed on the following day.

From that meeting patrol gets a heads up, but things would often change at night, and the groomers would notify the Director of Ski Patrol if they have any concerns with a particular run.

But apparently a sandwich was not on today's menu, because now he had to check on that injured skier who was being treated in the First Aid Room.

He got to the First Aid Room and encountered Bill Redmond doing paperwork in the snow safety office in the back. Bill filled him in on the injured skier, who'd been sent to the Driggs hospital via ambulance accompanied by one of his friends. Jon made sure all the appropriate forms had been filled out, including the blue index card that is filled in by the patient. Even a request for a band-aid needs to be accompanied by the blue index card, since patrol cannot "treat" anyone without it. The red tape of insurance regulations and resort policies was a pain, but it was part of the job and it was important to do it right.

Jon's radio crackled and he answered. It was Jared, one of his younger patrollers, asking him about a damaged trail sign over on Peaked. He also needed another piece of bamboo to mount it, and couldn't find any. Jon went to the storeroom to check the inventory, to see if more had to be ordered.

In the storeroom, he scanned the open cabinets for the replacement sign Jared had requested. There were only two left, unless Pete had a secret stash somewhere. He took one, and grabbed a bamboo pole to mount it on.

While some signs are mounted on bamboo poles, others use 2-by-2 wood posts, and still others are on 4-by-4 posts. The 2-by-2's are about eight feet tall before you stick them in the snow, and the 4-by-4's about twelve feet. The 'closed' signs, intended to prevent people from going out of bounds, are about 9-by-13, a little bigger than a car license plate. They're often mounted on bamboo. There are two notches built into the sign and the bamboo is fed through the notches, then the sign is slid down onto it.

Are there guidelines for how to space the poles? According to Pete Kerry, Ski Patrol Director in 2010, "[The spacing is] random. There is no set distance." Jon had trained many of the junior patrollers—just as he had been trained—emphasizing that every third pole should have a 'closed' sign mounted on it. Still, he knew that the mounted signs, unfortunately, were no match for the fierce winds coming down off the mountain. *Jon Alexander: "The wind blows signs, even the 4-by-4's, over at times."* The wind could also turn a sign, making it appear that the closed section is in a different direction.

During the afternoon sweeps the patrollers are checking for anyone still on the mountain after the lifts have closed. *Jon Alexander: "Based on the guidelines of how we created these sweeps they're required to follow as closely as they can based on snow conditions, travel conditions, weather—ski those routes looking for people that might still be on the hill, listening for people that might be on the hill, and we do a lot of yelling, calling out to see if people may be on the hill."*

Those who are patrolling a boundary are supposed to look out for tracks of persons who have crossed the boundary. Reporting those tracks to dispatch, however, is not required. *Jon Alexander: "We don't report it... hopefully [the patrollers] make a mental note of it."*

* * *

"It is common for lost skiers to have skied out-of-bounds. Some may attempt to climb back up to the point where they went out-of-bounds. However, ski boots make walking difficult and slow at best." —Lost Person Behavior by Robert J. Koester, p. 231

Eddie made his way over towards the ridge of the mountain, the furthest run from the lift. He was having the time of his life. It was snowing heavily and the fresh powder sprayed up around him during his descent. *Yes, this is the goods.* After having skied all day he was in his stride. It sometimes took him all day to really get going; it was as if his body had to remember how to ski every time.

Fred: *"By the end of the day he'd be romping down that thing."*

As was the practice in the Fitzgerald family, Eddie planned the last run of the day to be an easy one. It was the sandwich method—milk runs to start and also to end—keep challenging runs in the middle. That way you could warm up at the beginning of the day, and take it easy in the afternoon when you were tired. His dad had taught him to plan his skiing that way and he never varied from it; perhaps because of Asperger's Syndrome, Eddie was a creature of habit.

It was really true what they said about Targhee— there didn't seem to be anyone around, especially where he was now, to skier's far right of that double chair. There was something about skiing through glades—amongst trees—that made him feel particularly good. *Totally great. But this is going to be the last run, I don't want to miss the bus.*

This trip had been a nice opportunity to practice some of the techniques he'd learned the previous weekend. He'd worked on Gorilla Turns, using the whole body to force the turn; then some ruades, which are accomplished by lifting both ski tails and pivoting on the tips. He practiced some Christies, some carves, some swing turns, all the while trying to lock onto his skis' sweet spot so he could make the smoothest turns possible. Although his skis were actually more suited to groomed runs, he thought he was doing okay with them off piste.

Even with the bad visibility, Eddie felt comfortable practicing the fancier maneuvers. Way over here, he didn't have to worry about running into anybody because of not seeing them. Unlike the runs closer to the lift, this one seemed to be empty. No yodeling; his surroundings were totally silent except for the swoosh of his skis in the snow. Behind the clouds, the dimmed sun was bearing down on the tree line and the snowfall was tapering off.

He figured it was just about time to get back to base and catch the bus. He snowplowed, stopped and looked at his watch: 3:20 p.m.

Hey. Wait a minute. Shouldn't there be a traverse or something here? I should be parallel with the base right now. But there's nothing. Okay, it must just be a little further down.

He continued down the fall line of the mountain, but much slower this time. Instead of the pure enjoyment, the zen-like immersion he was capable of, he was now focused on getting to base. It would be a pain in the ass to miss the bus back to Jackson. He could always take the town bus, but half the fun was riding on the bus with all the ski group people.

Shit, it's 3:35, I might miss it. Where the hell is that traverse? Base should be to the left, but I don't see any traverse. He dialed Mario again, and again the call went to voicemail. He pulled the Grand Targhee trail map out of the pocket of his red Coolar jacket and opened it. *Yes, I came down this Powder Cache run close to the ridge ... that's the boundary there, the North Boundary Traverse. What the hell? This boundary wasn't on the map next to the lift! This is a different map! I've gotta be below the boundary now, well below it. There should've been a rope line there. Where the hell was the rope line? There was no rope, no signs... is that possible, there's no rope?* He suddenly felt nauseous. He took off his gloves and held them between his knees, fished a used paper napkin from breakfast—that was hours ago—out of his pants pocket and blew his nose, and spit into the snow. He brought the map closer to his face. *I must be down here. I'm definitely below the base. The cross country section is to the west... if I could get to that ...* He took out his cellphone again, but now there was no signal. And now the battery was way down. Way, way down.

Okay, I'm going to miss the bus. Accept it. Now I have to concentrate on getting back to base. It will take a hell of a long time to hike out, lugging my skis. Damn it. He looked at his cell phone again. Still no signal. He powered off the phone.

There's got to be a traverse nearby. But I don't know the area and it's hard to see. Maybe there's a call box, I could call ski patrol. But I don't think I'm even in the resort now. There probably aren't any call boxes out here. There were no groomed trails to be seen, and no cat tracks. There was nothing but snow, pine trees, distant peaks shrouded with mist. It was going to be dark soon. But at least the snowfall seemed to be abating. He scanned the snow-covered slope for any signs of tracks from other skiers or snowboarders. *Nobody out here but me.* Looking back uphill, he noticed some irregularities in the snow, slightly outlined by the fading daylight. He side-stepped back up the hill until he saw what seemed to be a snowmobile track.

If I follow the snowmobile track, that might lead to a road or some kind of exit out of here. Plus, if I go up a little ways, I might be able to get a signal on my phone. He unclicked his boots from the skis and put them under his left arm. He took both his ski poles in his right hand. He took a deep breath for the uphill hike, which wouldn't be easy in ski boots, carrying his skis. But it seemed to him like the best option.

Eddie trudged back up the mountain. Post holing along the snowmobile track, he turned back periodically to see if there was any sign of human activity. He decided to check the phone again. At 3:54 p.m. he pulled it out, powered it on, and was elated to see one bar of signal on the screen.

Who should I call? Mario again? Fred? Larry? No, what could they do. They don't know where the hell I am any more than I do. I only have maybe a few minutes of battery left. I could call the resort, here's their number on the back of the map ... but if I'm outside of the resort now ... better cut right to the chase and call 911. Damn it! This is embarrassing! Why is this happening? This never happens! Not to me!

The grey light of dusk had tinted the scene around him to a dull pewter patina. The contours of the slope were less visible now, only the trees marked the terrain beneath the surface. He steeled himself to dial the three numbers that are engraved in every city-dweller's brain: 911. The last resort.

911 was for emergencies. It was not to be abused or taken lightly, and Eddie did not take it so. He hated to bother them, actually. But daylight was fading fast, and things were beginning to look serious. He pressed the three numbers on his phone and held it to his ear.

He heard it ring; a feeble ring, interrupted ... severed by staccato silences ... then a click. Disconnected. And again—no signal. He waited a few minutes and checked again. *Yes! One bar!* Once more he dialed. Once more he heard the weak ringing that was immediately cut off.

Tesha Wilson, 911 operator, Driggs ID: "There are fewer towers in our area and we will frequently get dropped calls or a number will ring and you answer and there is nobody there. That frequently would happen."

Eddie looked up, scanning the upper part of the mountain. *I'll go a little farther up. If I got a signal here, I can probably get a better one a little higher.* He began to climb once more, carrying his skis and post-holing along the snowmobile track. It was an effort to walk like this, especially in this altitude. But his legs could handle it, they were well-trained. After fifteen minutes or so he decided to give his phone another try. It gave him the time, 4:13 p.m. But it would not give him what he needed most—a connection to a 911 operator.

Shit. This is unbelievable. Okay, get a grip Eddie. This approach is obviously not working. So go back down the mountain. It has to level out at some point. Then I'll be able to get to a road. Yeah. Let's do that.

* * *

View Enhancing (from Chapter 5, Lost Person Strategies), Lost Person Behavior by Robert Koester: "Unable to find anything familiar after traveling around the woods, the lost person attempts to gain a position of height to view landmarks in the distance. This person attempts to enhance his view by climbing a hill, ridge, or tree... With the advent of cell phones more lost subjects use view enhancement. However, instead of moving uphill to obtain a view, they gain elevation in an attempt to obtain a cell tower signal. Lost subjects will leave trails and other travel aids and often head directly uphill."

Patroller Kris Hart was doing the afternoon sweep off the Blackfoot lift. Along the way his duties included calling out periodically that the mountain was closing. He began about 4:15 p.m. at the patrol station at the summit of Fred's Mountain, skied northward across the top of Sitting Bull Ridge to the Headwall Traverse to the end; then down the top of Chief Joe Bowl briefly, turning onto the Blackfoot Traverse that goes above the Blackfoot chairlift. He continued out the Blackfoot Traverse, moving out to above Powder Cache where it meets the rope line on the ridge. He traversed back in a southerly direction to Raven Wood, then turned back to the north, making a crossing that finished at the northern end of the North Boundary Traverse. At one point he noticed a track leaving the resort boundary. It appeared to be a snowboarder track. He had often seen tracks at that boundary, usually made by skiers and boarders looking for fresh powder. He was not required to report tracks leaving the boundary. Kris rarely did anything he wasn't required to do.

Patroller Mandy Jones: *"It was quite often that folks would make the mistake of leaving the North Boundary Traverse and getting out there and realizing they weren't headed back to base area and not coming across any other groomed terrain. So we frequently got people going down there via ski or snowboard and then having to climb or hike back out."*

From the North Boundary Traverse, Kris went to just above the bottom terminal of Blackfoot, where he waited for the wave-off from the other patrollers. Then he took the Little Beaver Traverse to the bottom of the Shoshone lift, where the sweep was complete. His day over, he went to the locker room to change and store his gear. His locker was next to Jared's, who walked in right after him.

"Hey Kris," Jared said in greeting, pulling off his knit cap and shaking snow off it. "You coming down to the Common House to eat?"

"No, I can't. Got something to do."

"Okay. I think Andrew and Mandy and Cathy are going, if you change your mind. Or else see ya tomorrow."

"Have fun, Dude. Later," Kris replied, slamming his locker shut and grabbing his backpack. He couldn't wait to see his girlfriend.

* * *

The paramedics wheeled Mario up the ramp of the emergency room of the Teton Valley Health Care hospital in Driggs, Idaho. Freddie really needed to find the men's room, but he continued to follow the gurney, not wanting to leave Mario alone.

Gabe Mender was the ER nurse that day. Gabe was a young man, slight of build with reddish brown hair, and an avid skier. He realized immediately Mario had a multiple in-boot fracture, and he tried not to wince.

Mender: "It was a bad fracture and it needed surgery for sure. But he actually refused to get it fixed there; he refused our orthopedic doctor."

Mario: "They put a splinter [sic] on me. I don't know why they did that. They should have put a cast on me being I was going to stay at Wyoming for another five days. You know, they wanted me to go home or we can do an operation over here. I said, 'What, are you out of your mind doing an operation over here? And then I have to go home all by myself? It doesn't make any sense.' ... They should have put a cast on my leg. It would have been better for me. I had to walk on the tarmac, walk on the snow, climb the stairs..."

The splint applied to Mario's left leg is known as an Orthoplast splint. The Orthoplast material is ideal for temporary splints and braces because it can be molded to any shape by heating it. Despite Mario's insistence that a cast would have been better for him, many orthopedic surgeons feel that applying a cast too soon after an injury does more harm than good.

Thomas N. Joseph, MD: "You cannot put a patient who just had an injury into a cast, in most circumstances. Because if swelling were to occur, there's no place for it to go. It will compress the blood vessels and it will compress the nerves, and you'll have permanent damage. So that is not something you'd want to do... so, initial injury [calls for a] splint. And then later on you can go into a cast when the swelling has reduced."

Mario: "They said, 'If you really want to get through this, we will do an operation. We have the best.' I mean, I guess they got the best doctors there being there are sports injuries from the mountain. But no insurance, and they told me right off the bat just for the operation, thirty-five, forty thousand dollars. 'Where are you coming from? Where am I going to get that kind of money, really?'"

"Freddie," said Mario from the gurney, "I gotta get the skis back to that place we rented from. You know ... the place in Teton Village." His speech was slow and slurred; the strong painkillers he'd been given were taking effect.

Freddie shook his head. "Don't even think about that now, man. We'll take care of it for you. You should just rest, don't get agitated."

"Why am I so, like, injury prone?" asked Mario of no one in particular. "I'm always banging here and banging there," he mumbled. Freddie could hardly understand him now, Mario was so out of it.

Freddie shrugged. "I dunno, I guess that's just you. Shit. But you know what? I just thought of something my grandpa used to say."

"Yeah?" replied Mario sleepily.

"He used to say, 'everything that has a beginning has an ending.' So, I don't know, I guess when bad stuff happens you have to realize it will end at some point."

Mario smiled weakly. "Yeah. Like life."

"Yeah, right," said Freddie. He heard a vibrating sound and turned his head to hear where it was coming from. The source was Mario's jacket, draped over a chair in the corner of the room. Must be his cellphone.

"Mario, should I answer your phone?" There was no reply. Mario was drifting in and out, mercifully, because the pain must have been excruciating. Freddie went over to the jacket to check who was calling, but the ringing stopped and there was no display on the screen. Well, it didn't really matter. Mario wasn't going to be taking any calls for awhile.

* * *

The large bus and the minivan were idling in the parking lot of Grand Targhee. Exhaust smoke from their respective tailpipes hovered in the pre-twilight. Forty six LISG people stood around in the snowy parking lot next to the buses. The couple not staying at the Parkway Inn had already left for their friends' home.

Marco and Ross stood off to one side, quietly discussing the situation. They had heard that the small van would be going to the hospital to pick up Mario.

"If we go with Fred to the hospital," said Marco, "we might be there all night."

Ross shook his head. "I don't think so. If they do an operation or something, where Mario has to stay in the hospital, we'd just go back to Jackson. Anyway," he continued, "it's not like a crowded New York hospital. Like, they can decide whatever they're going to do right away. There won't be a line of people waiting."

Marco kicked some snow. "Well, some of us have to go to the hospital, because there's not enough room on the big bus for everyone. We may not have a choice."

"Yeah, but you know who's going. Fred, definitely. That guy George and his son. Probably Rich and Cheryl."

Their conversation was interrupted by Fred, who raised his arms up and called, "Listen up everyone, please." He cleared his throat. The conversations ceased and everyone turned to look at Fred. "Everybody can get back on the bus you came on, but when we reach Driggs we're gonna pull over and switch some people over to the big bus. Then we're gonna take the van to the hospital and go get Mario. So let's stuff as much gear as we can in the big bus, okay?" There was a general nodding of consensus, and the boarding of the buses began.

Once everyone was seated, Fred stepped up into the coach bus and scanned the heads of the passengers. He had the worst headache ever. He had downed a couple of Johnny Walker's back at the bar, but they didn't help, not with anything. This was the worst disaster ever to have happened on one of his trips. And to happen to Mario, his closest friend!

"Is everyone here," Fred called out despondently. There were a couple jovial replies, some sarcastic replies and in general a lackluster response from the group. Everyone was feeling the day's activities, and Mario's injury had cast a pall on their usually upbeat mood. "Okay," said Fred, stepping off the bus. He went over to the van and got in the front passenger seat. He looked at the driver. "Let's go," he said.

Once on Rt. 33, heading south into the deepening twilight, the buses drove to just before the turnoff for the airport and pulled off to the side of the road. Most of those who had ridden in the minivan got off and switched over to the large bus. It was pretty much standing room only with all the gear and the passengers already on the bus, so the newcomers grabbed onto overheads and seat backs in preparation for the rest of the ride back to Jackson.

In the minivan seven passengers besides Fred remained, leaving the front bench seat clear for Mario. In another five minutes they were making a left onto Howard Avenue and pulling into the Teton Valley Hospital parking lot. "Hey guys," Fred addressed the group, "I'll just go in, you can wait here for us okay?" He stepped out into the dry Idaho evening; the snowfall had ended but the clouds lingered, darkening the dusk so that it seemed later than it really was.

Fred looked at his watch—not even 5:00 and he was exhausted already. He approached the reception desk and was directed to a recovery room adjacent to the Emergency Room, where Mario was resting after being outfitted with his Orthoplast splint by ER nurse Gabe Mender.

Fred: "They were really good about it. The doctor said, 'Listen, Fred, if he wants to fly home, here is my number. Call me and I will call the airline and say this guy has a serious injury, he has to go right now.' But Mario didn't want to go home. I was worried about Mario because he had quit his job to take care of his mother. I have known him for 25 years, so I said, wow, how is he going to take care of his mom if he is in bed. She is like 95 years old."

* * *

Eddie continued to posthole his way back down the mountain, following the tracks he'd made on the way up. When he got to the point where he had stopped before, he stood there for a few minutes, thinking. *Should I put my skis back on? It's going to be dark soon and I don't want to ski off a cliff. But if I'm going to go to the bottom of the mountain, it would take a long time to posthole it. Plus I'd be dragging my skis. If my cell dies before I get through to 911, my best bet is getting down to a road and hiking out. Let's see... okay, let me ski down a little ways, while I can still see where I'm going. Then when it's too dark to see I'll posthole it if I have to. But hopefully I'll reach 911 before that.* He clicked into his skis once more, looking at his watch before continuing. It was 5:04.

Eddie was right: the resort boundary to the north hadn't been shown on the map that was posted at the top of the mountain. But when he pulled out the pocket trail map, Eddie realized that the blowup map at the top had been taken from the map inset, not the main map, and showed a different orientation.

The boundary that Eddie crossed is called the North Boundary Traverse. It is a groomed snowcat road that cuts directly across the skier's path, following the Powder Cache Trail down Fred's Mountain. Powder Cache is the trail farthest away from the lift. If skiers do not make that hard left when reaching the North Boundary Traverse, they end up having to hike back up the mountain—in their ski boots—to get back inside the resort. Not fun.

Because of its location at the far edge of Grand Targhee, Powder Cache does not get skied nearly as often as the other trails. That goes double for foggy days when visibility is barely a few feet in front of you. The navigationally-challenged among us naturally prefer to ski closer to the main part of the resort so as not to get lost. Eddie may have been autistic, but he was not navigationally-challenged. On the contrary. He knew maps, and he trusted his unerring sense of direction.

***Letter from Ed Fitzgerald Sr.:** "Let's just surmise, nobody was skiing Powder Cache that afternoon but Eddie. (I can't tell you how many times I've been the only skier on a trail and been uncertain of the way down due to snow, fog, rain or whatever. In most resort type skiing you do your best to get to the bottom and VOILA! There's the bar! Time to celebrate.) Late in the day ... this particular day ...*

there's no one else on your part of the mountain. You don't know the mountain ... you don't know the trail ... you can't see ... you follow the fall line ... you take your skis off because you know you're in trouble. Why doesn't every skier get lost? Better conditions ... better local knowledge ... BETTER LUCK. He made a mistake skiing that particular part of the mountain that particular time of the day. HE AND I FOLLOWED A PARTICULAR PATTERN. MAKE YOUR LAST RUN AN EASY ONE. I THINK HE THOUGHT HE WAS DOING THAT BECAUSE HE HAD SKIED THE OTHER TRAILS FROM BLACKFOOT EARLIER. HE MISJUDGED THE WEATHER AND THE TERRAIN. I do know the Blackfoot lift was a secondary one on the mountain. Old, slow double chair, vs. high speed quads on the two major trails. Un-groomed poorly marked trails. Trees. And when you get to Powder Cache ... danger! Probably the trail you ski in good conditions in good weather ... not late in the day ... poor light, foggy. Don't underestimate the issue of poor light along with fog and snow. That's why the locals call the mountain OLD FOGGY."

One would think that Targhee's North Boundary Traverse would be a no-brainer hard closure. A rope line, signs, the works. And now, it is. But when Eddie Cola skied at Targhee in 2010, the rope hadn't been up for years. It had been removed by Ski Patrol Director Pete Kerry's predecessor, and had never been replaced. The reason given, according to Kerry, was that "they considered it a hazard for clotheslining people coming down from up above." After the removal of that rope line at the North Boundary Traverse, the only indication that the other side of the traverse was out of bounds would have been the "closed" signs, spaced out at random intervals on bamboo poles. Whether those signs could be seen or not depended on visibility conditions.

Pete Kerry: "We had people that would go off that cat track and realize they weren't in the right spot, so they walked back up."

* * *

Testimony Of Expert Witness Dick Penniman:

"As one enters the Powder Cache area from the end of the Blackfoot Traverse road, the terrain and vegetation blocks [sic] the North Boundary Traverse road far below from view. As one descends down through the trees and into the open, however, portions of the road become visible but are not obvious unless one knows the road is there. In many places, dense trees were left immediately uphill of the road, blocking it from view entirely to within only a few feet. On the other hand, as one comes into the open portions of the Powder Cache area, the entire slope down to Rick's Basin is visible and obvious giving the appearance of one long continuous powder slope. Mr. Fitzgerald's ski tracks were located immediately adjacent to one of the groups of trees that blocked the view of the road from above.

Throughout the in-bounds open terrain of the Grand Targhee Mountain Resort, numerous groomed traverse roads cross open slopes. It is not uncommon to ski across these traverse roads numerous times during the course of the day. In fact, it would be unusual not to cross several of these traverse roads if one is skiing the popular, ungroomed, powder slopes for which the resort is renowned. But for the rope line on the North Boundary Traverse road [which was not up on January 19, 2010] the continuous appearance of the Powder Cache terrain would give no indication that this road is any different than any of the many other traverse roads that one crosses throughout the resort. The road, by itself, would give no indication that it is the boundary to closed terrain.

Even though it is permanently closed to patrons, the area below the North Boundary Traverse road known as Rick's Basin is within the U.S. Forest Service permit area of the Grand Targhee Mountain Resort. From personal knowledge the slopes of Rick's Basin consist mostly of open or sparsely treed, low angle and inviting powder terrain. However, there is no chairlift access back up for those who venture down. A large trail map sign at the top of the Blackfoot chairlift clearly shows the resort boundary continuing along the ridge of Fred's Mountain, past the beginning of the

North Boundary Traverse road down to the bottom flats of Rick's Basin. No closure is evident at the North Boundary Traverse on this map. Anyone reading it would naturally conclude that clearly the entire slope of the Powder Cache area down to and including Rick's Basin is open terrain. Even the testimony of ski patrol personnel during their depositions admitted that, indeed, what the map showed is incorrect. Prior to their depositions, none of the patrollers had realized that this map gave false and misleading information. It is not known if Mr. Fitzgerald looked at this map for direction before he skied down to the Powder Cache slopes, but [it] is conceivable that he did because he was new to and unfamiliar with the Grand Targhee Mountain Resort. If he had depended on this map, there is no reason that Mr. Fitzgerald would have expected or been on the lookout for a closure line at the North Boundary Traverse road. He would have approached it as he would any of the many other traverse roads he already would have encountered earlier that day."

* * *

Down the street from the hospital, 911 Senior Dispatcher Tesha Wilson had just finished her 9-to-5 shift at the Teton County Idaho Sheriff's Office in Driggs. She was dog tired, but she couldn't go home just yet because a dispatcher's meeting had been called by her boss, Viola Walls. It would probably take around an hour and a half. After that, she planned to rush home since she had to be back at work again at 7 a.m.

Tesha hadn't been getting much sleep lately. Her 20 year old son was on her mind a lot; he'd fallen in with a bad crowd and she suspected he was involved in a string of robberies that had taken place over the last month. She didn't want to see her son in trouble with the law. Not only would it be unfortunate for him, but it would also reflect badly on her, since she worked for the Sheriff's Department. She hoped that somehow he might straighten himself out, though it didn't seem likely.

Tesha's relief in the dispatch office was the new guy, Mark Silver, who was on swing shift. He'd only been hired five months before and was green as a 911 dispatcher. He was not even Level 1 certified yet. But he'd learn, just as Tesha had learned. Like most professions, dispatching was one best learned on the job. It was impossible to totally prepare for the various emergencies that would arise because every call was different. And the 911 dispatchers fielded not only emergency phone calls, but they also dispatched for normal events, traffic, and other non-emergency situations.

The dispatchers meeting was to be held at 5:30 in the training room, which was a few steps down the hall from the dispatch room. The training room was large and could accommodate around eighty people. It was a former courtroom that had been renovated into a conference room; the benches had been removed, replaced by tables and chairs. Since there were never more than two dispatchers working the same shift, these occasional meetings were a way for everyone to touch base and make sure things were running smoothly.

Viola Walls had been Administrative Director of Operations for the Teton County Idaho Sheriff's Office for four and a half years. In addition to her POST (Peace Officer Standards & Training) certification in communications, she was certified in IC (Incident Command) Structure, as a Public Information Officer, and Property and Evidence Specialist. And in her additional capacity as Emergency Medical Dispatch, she would give pre-arrival instructions to callers before the Fire Department or EMS arrived on the scene. Her office was right next to the training room, and across the hall, kitty-corner, from dispatch. Viola supervised a team of six dispatchers, including Tesha, Mark Silver, and Sharon Courier, who would be relieving Mark at 11 p.m. Being on swing shift, Mark had started his shift at 5 p.m. and would remain until midnight. He would not be able to attend the meeting since he was on duty. Viola knew Mark really should not be working alone since he was not yet certified. Budget constraints, however, superseded that technicality.

Because the dispatch room was in the same building as the Sheriff's Office, Teton County Idaho Sheriff Lichevy dropped in quite often. He did so on this evening, going up the stairs to the second floor where dispatch and the training room were located. Teton County Idaho Search and Rescue Commander Terry Diamond followed right after the sheriff, and poked his head into the dispatch room.

"Hello Sheriff, hello Terry," Mark said, turning briefly toward the door before going back to monitoring the radio communications on the console. He tried to appear especially diligent whenever he thought his boss Viola, or the Sheriff, or the SAR commander might be watching him.

The 911 console was laid out in two sections on either side of the dispatcher. There were three computer screens at each station. The console system was manufactured by a company called Moducom; it provided the dispatcher with access to fire and police radio traffic, landline and cell phone calls, and the ability to communicate with multiple people simultaneously. The dispatcher could use a headset with attached microphone, or the external speakers with a countertop mic and a foot pedal. 911 calls that came in were recorded by the Moducom system, and could be played back as often as necessary by the dispatcher. *Mark Silver: "We will do it frequently depending on the type of call. It's a tool that we use to help us gather information if the call has been disconnected, to go back and listen or to just verify information."*

As the dispatcher fields radio traffic and incoming calls, he or she is trained to type into the CAD, or Computer Automated Dispatch system. Each entry receives a time stamp, noting the time the entry was made by the dispatcher. *Sharon Courier: "You were trained to type every word the minute you heard it."* But what happens when there's only one dispatcher on duty, and there are a lot of calls? *Mark Silver: "You multitask. You just do the best to keep up."*

* * *

Larry was quite pleased with himself. He had found a fantastic leather belt with a large, oval silver buckle in one of the shops in the Jackson town square. It was a bit expensive but he bought it anyway, forgoing the cowboy hat in favor of the belt. He had walked all over town and come back to the Parkway in the afternoon to take a nice long Jacuzzi, and then a nap. His roommate was apparently out skiing so he had the room to himself.

He was woken from his nap by his cellphone. He reached for it on the nightstand and squinted at the incoming number, which he didn't recognize. "Hello?"

"Larry, it's Fred."

"Hey Fred. Did you finally buy a cellphone?"

"Uh, no, it's Freddie's ... Larry. Listen. There's been an accident."

Larry threw the blanket off and sprang upright. "Whoa, what? What happened?"

"It's Mario. He broke his leg. It's pretty bad. I'm at the hospital now. Jesus Christ. It's really bad."

"Ahhhhh, shit! Are they putting a cast on him or what?"

"No, I don't know, right now he's got some kind of splint thing or something. Listen, we're gonna bring him back to the hotel, but he won't be able to walk around that good. You know, he's gonna need some help. Could you ... do you think you could switch rooms and stay with Mario, help him out?"

"Yeah, sure! Where are you? When are you getting here?"

"Probably like an hour or something. Isn't the other bus back yet?"

"I don't know, I don't think so. Okay, I'll be here, yeah. Tell Mario I'll come down and stay in his room with him and help him out, no problem."

As Larry pressed the end call button, he realized Fred's voice had sounded very strained. Well, no wonder—Mario breaking his leg, that was tough. But it was part of skiing. Almost expected, at some point. Larry was glad he hadn't gone with them today, it probably would've been *him* who would've broken some bone or other. He swung his legs over the edge of the bed and put on his socks. It was going to be a long night.

As Larry was getting dressed, most of the ski group was downstairs in front of the hotel, sorting whose gear was whose as they unloaded it from the bus. Cheryl and Rich found their skis pretty quickly because they had been amongst the last to stow them. They themselves had ridden in the minivan until it was time to switch over to the big bus to make room for Mario.

"Hey—in a few hours it'll be your birthday," Cheryl whispered to Rich.

Rich put his arm around her. "Yeah, but it's not starting out that great," he replied. He didn't know Mario well, but it certainly was a letdown that one of their group had been hurt. Every time a skier is injured, it's a reminder to his or her companions of that old saying, "there but for the grace of God go I."

Cheryl nodded. "I know. Poor Mario, I feel so bad for him! But I still want you to have a good birthday. Let's go out to a nice dinner tonight, just us," she suggested.

Rich nodded. "Great idea honey." They took their gear and went up to their room on the second floor. As Rich was taking a shower, Cheryl sat on the bed and perused the restaurant choices in the Jackson Hole tourist guide. She rubbed her legs. Where was that bottle of Advil she'd bought at Targhee? She pawed through her purse and found it, thought about taking three but took two instead. A bottle of wine at dinner would take the rest of the edge off. And she was definitely, positively, not going skiing tomorrow.

* * *

Eddie felt his heartbeat racing. It was getting dark. His cell phone was dying. He hadn't the faintest idea where he was, he felt completely turned around. What would happen if he couldn't find his way out of here? It was cold out, and it would only get colder after the sun went down completely. He pushed up the sleeve of his red Coolar jacket with his gloved hand. His watch read 5:37. In less than two hours it would be dark. He shivered. *This is insane! This is like, a bad dream or something. Okay Eddie, calm down. Just get yourself to a road and you'll be okay. Keep following the fall line down, it has to lead to a road.* He was walking, dragging his equipment. At this point it was really too dark to be skiing. He didn't know the terrain and could easily ski off a cliff. *Everybody's probably eating dinner now. They have to realize I'm not there. Mario will know I'm not there, at least. Maybe they went to different places to eat, and everybody thinks I'm with another group. Shit, if I could just make a phone call! Maybe there's a tower further down.*

* * *

Larry gazed out the window in the lobby while he waited for the van carrying Fred, Freddie, the injured Mario, and the few other ski club folks who'd been able to fit in the van with Mario aboard. The sun had already set, and the streetlights shining through the cloudy evening gave the snow on the ground a bluish-yellow tinge.

Finally, around 7 p.m. the van pulled up to the Parkway Inn. Larry tossed on his jacket and went out to meet them. Fred eased himself down from the passenger seat, opening the side door of the van. Mario was taking up the entire first bench, his leg propped up on the seat and the hospital crutches on the floor next to him. He passed the crutches out to Larry, and Fred and the driver helped him get out of the van.

"Mario, how you doing?" Larry asked, helping him position the crutches under his arms.

"Not great my friend," Mario replied with a thin smile. He steadied himself on the crutches and tried a few steps as he kept his injured left leg up off the ground.

"Listen, let's get you to your room, come on," said Fred. He and Larry walked on either side of Mario, Fred carrying the injured man's backpack.

"I'm your new roommate," Larry told Mario. "So whatever you need, I'll help you. Okay buddy?"

"Thanks Larry," Mario said.

As they crossed the threshold into the inn, Mackenzie Ryder saw what was going on and came out from behind the desk. "Oh, my goodness! I'm so sorry!" she exclaimed. She didn't know Mario's name but knew his face well since the LISG had been staying there for four days thus far. "If there's anything I can do, please let me know," she said sincerely.

"Thanks. We're not really sure what we might need just yet, but we'll let you know," said Larry. The three of them walked slowly to the room. Larry took the key from Mario and opened the door. The room had been made up, so the first thing Larry did was loosen the bedclothes on the first bed so Mario could move around in it a little easier.

"I know," said Larry, "you need some extra pillows, that's what you need. Then you can prop your leg up. I'll go tell that girl." He went back out to the lobby, leaving Fred alone with Mario.

"Shit, Fred," Mario said after Larry had gone, "I never should have gone up that last run. I couldn't see a thing up there! I should have known better."

"I know, I know. It was bad visibility. It's not your fault. Here, do you want to sit in the chair, or lie on the bed?"

Mario uttered a sound that was somewhere between a groan and a sigh. "The bed, I guess." He sat down on the edge and Fred took the crutches from him, leaning them against the wall. He helped Mario lift his splinted left leg onto the bed. They sat together on the bed in silence for a minute or two, until Larry returned with three pillows under his arm.

"Here, let's put the leg up on a couple of these." Larry adjusted the pillows carefully under Mario's leg. "Did the doctor give you any pain meds?"

"Yeah," said Mario, "they're in a bottle in that bag."

Fred opened the knapsack and found the small blue bottle, handing it to Mario.

Larry went into the bathroom and filled a coffee cup with water. Handing it to Mario, he said, "Hey, I have to go get my stuff from my room, I'll be right back, okay?" He left the room to retrieve his suitcase. He had already tossed everything into it in preparation for changing rooms.

Fred sat on the edge of the bed with Mario, who reached over and grabbed the TV remote and began scrolling through the channels with the sound muted.

"Looks like movie night," said Fred.

"Yup."

Fred gazed at the screen mindlessly while Mario worked the remote, lingering on a John Wayne movie for a few moments before resting the remote back on the nightstand. Larry returned with his suitcase. "What do you want to eat Mario? I'll go to the diner and bring back some food."

"Hey Larry," said Fred, "could you pick up something for me too? Maybe a cheeseburger and fries or something?"

"Sure. What do you want Mario?"

"I dunno, the same as Fred I guess. And a Coke."

"Hey," said Fred, "while you're getting the grub, I'm gonna go change my clothes. I'll be right back." He left the room and went across the hall to his own room. He was still wearing his ski clothing, but he was so tired that just the thought of changing was too much to deal with. *I'll just lie down for a minute, then I'll change, eat dinner* ... He took off his shoes and lay down on the bed. *Just for a minute.* A few moments later he was sound asleep.

Eddie and sister Christine, ages 2 & 3

Eddie & Christine, Jones Beach

Eddie with his mother Gail and his grandfather

Eddie (age 23) and Carla

Eddie with Ed Sr. and "Rags"

Eddie (age 29), Christine & Ed Sr.

Eddie (far right) with ski pals in the Alps

Eddie in Queens, NY apt.

Eddie and ski group celebrating.

Chapter 4
The Night Of January 19

Mark Silver: "He made mention of being near some trees and there was some unintelligible words that I could not understand."

Mark Silver was glad to have a job. Dispatching over the radio and fielding 911 emergency calls made him feel important. He felt his job was even sort of glamorous, even though it was behind-the-scenes.

After graduating from Teton High School, he had not gone to college. Instead, he had flirted with various jobs while still living at his parents' house. This dispatcher job had enabled him to move out and get his own apartment, although the pay was not great, only about $16 an hour. His plan was to get fully certified so he could get a promotion and earn more. The most experienced dispatchers made between $17 and $25 an hour.

Mark's empire was a large desk with three computer monitors mounted on it. There was a microphone on a gooseneck stand and a foot pedal, or the dispatcher could wear an earphone and mic set instead. The desk had a landline telephone, and the room had shelves with notebooks full of access numbers that may be needed by the dispatcher on duty. There was a large calendar on the wall, and some photos and memos on a bulletin board.

Mark had begun his training five months previously, starting with a two-week course run by his boss, Viola Walls. He had passed his probationary period, but was not yet certified for 911 Level 1 dispatching. Nevertheless, due to Teton County Idaho budget constraints, there was not always another dispatcher available to assist Silver. He often covered a shift by himself.

January 19, 2010 was a Tuesday. Usually mid-week incidents were fewer than weekend incidents, but because this was the end of the Martin Luther King holiday weekend, there was a bit more happening than on your typical Tuesday night. *Mark Silver: "On top of [Eddie Fitzgerald's] call [there were] several other events and other phone calls I would have had to field."* When Sheriff Lichevy and then Terry Diamond had walked by the dispatch room, Mark barely had time to acknowledge them.

The Sheriff and Terry Diamond, Commander of Teton County Idaho Search and Rescue, were on their way to a meeting of new SAR recruits. The meeting was set for 7 p.m. in the training room, immediately after the 911 dispatchers finished their regular staff meeting. The new recruits waited in the hallway until the dispatchers vacated the room.

Terry Diamond was a large man, dark-haired and mustached, who was rarely seen without a cowboy hat. He felt relieved to see so many people there because it's not easy to find recruits for SAR. It is a big time commitment, requiring the training sessions and at least one Saturday per month for mock rescue training, in addition to being available 24/7 to assist in whatever incidents might come up. *Terry Diamond: "We train for everything. We do swift water training. We do what we call ground pounding training, which means we're just walking on foot. We do four-wheeler training. We do snowmobile training... We practice the Incident Command System."*

All the Teton County Idaho SAR positions, including that of Commander, are voluntary. Who volunteers for a Search and Rescue team? Outdoor sports enthusiasts make up a large percentage, but there are also those who participate on the administrative end. Motivated by adventure and the satisfaction gained by helping others, SAR volunteers range in age from twenty to over seventy. Search and Rescue teams are often overseen by the Sheriff's Department, and work closely with law enforcement personnel in addition to medical professionals.

Diamond was a paramedic, not a skier. Originally from California, he moved to Idaho and came to Search and Rescue via his background in law enforcement—he's a graduate of the California Police Officers Academy, and served as Deputy Sheriff with Teton County Idaho from 1995 to 2001.

Diamond: "I walked in one night and paid the $20 dues and I was a member of Search and Rescue." Because of the difficulty in finding volunteers who are able to make the required time commitment for training and missions, SAR positions are frequently assigned according to which volunteers have the most flexible day jobs. Because he had the most flexible schedule— his day job as a bail bondsman allowed him to easily rearrange his work schedule— Diamond became the Commander of Teton County Idaho SAR.

"We request applications. We make sure they pass the background check we submit to the Sheriff's Office. And we sit down and interview candidates. Mostly what we're looking for [is] if they have the time commitment to volunteer for search and rescue."

But Teton County Idaho Search and Rescue is not the star of the show in Teton County. That reputation belongs to Teton County Wyoming's team. Wyoming performs over sixty rescue operations a year, compared with Idaho's fifteen to twenty. Idaho's equipment consists of a beat-up pickup truck and trailer and a couple of snowmobiles. Wyoming has tons of equipment. They have more money. They have more volunteers, and a paid Commander/Coordinator position that was filled by Don Oscar, a grumpy man whose aloof attitude didn't endear him to many people—people like Oscar's boss Sheriff Jennings, for example.

Oscar's duties as the SAR coordinator for Teton County Wyoming were to maintain, purchase and research the equipment, work on the budget, keep training records and mission records, assist with the 35 or so training directors and SAR team members, assist with grants, speak to the press, participate in search missions, and serve as a contact person for the organization, its members and its associated agencies. ***Don Oscar: "I also work for the board [of directors], which also is my boss because the board knows search and rescue they direct me as to daily operations."*** Oscar's office was situated in the Search and Rescue building on the south side of town.

Wyoming has the cachet that Idaho lacks, right down to celebrity volunteers: Harrison Ford has piloted his Bell 407 aircraft as a volunteer in at least two mountain rescues. The October 2007 edition of The Land Report gave details of one of these rescues, in which a lost and disoriented female hiker boarded the aircraft and immediately vomited into a rescuer's cap. Once safely on the ground, the starstruck victim remarked "I can't believe I barfed in Harrison Ford's helicopter!"

The proximity of Grand Targhee to the Wyoming-Idaho border, however, frequently puts lost guests in the vicinity of Idaho rather than Wyoming. Just to get to the resort, one must pass through Idaho. Indeed, there had been a number of incidents over the years where Targhee guests had ended up in Idaho's South Leigh Canyon, well past the northern boundary of the Grand Targhee Resort in Alta, Wyoming. Eddie "Cola" Fitzgerald was certainly not the first to have done so. One hopes, however, he will have been the last.

In New York City, one occasionally hears natives explain why they don't venture far from their home, downtown in the Village:

"I get the bends above 14th Street," they say. Similarly, Wyoming residents aren't often to be found exploring the territory to the west and north. *Don Oscar: "I would not say I have intimate knowledge of the Idaho side of the Tetons."* No, the people who are familiar with the backcountry of South Leigh Canyon are not from Wyoming. They are from Idaho.

* * *

Katrina Reagan, Front Desk Switchboard Operator, Grand Targhee Resort: "On the evening of Tuesday, January 19, 2010, close to the 8 p.m. hour I received a phone call at the front desk switchboard from the Teton County Idaho Sheriff's Office (I think his name was Mark). He informed me that we had a lost skier on the mountain and checked with me to see if he was a lodging guest with Grand Targhee. I told him he was not, he said the proper authorities from our resort had been notified and said that Search and Rescue from Teton County Idaho would be coming up to help with the search. (I was told this is because SAR from Idaho was meeting close by so they were together and available.) He also told me the caller mentioned they had been on a two-chair lift (I knew Blackfoot was the only one we had) and that he was lost somewhere in some kind of meadow. When I got off the phone, I informed Security (although I am not sure they believed me at first) and then proceeded to contact the Teton County Sheriff's Office in Wyoming (since we are their jurisdiction) to ensure that they were aware of the situation. She told me they were informed, we exchanged some info regarding the situation so everyone was on the same page, and she told me they were trying to contact someone from the Wyoming SAR as well.

I then received a call from Jon from Ski Patrol and he told me he was on his way up with about five patrollers to help out with the search. I contacted Security again to meet Ski Patrol when they got here and it was then the message was relayed to our groomers that were out and about.

The search then began with the patrollers, SAR and our groomers all helping. I remained at the FD with radios on to receive any necessary information and any phone calls from the switchboard. I packed up to leave a little after 10 p.m. (after completely filling in the night auditor who was taking my place) and then a call came in from one of the friends of the lost gentleman. The night auditor had taken his number and he was asking if anyone had been found yet. Not hearing the whole conversation, I took the number and contacted the friend back to get clothing descriptions and any other information that could be pertinent to the situation. The friend had told me he had spoken with SAR and given them that information and I simply told him I was ensuring this was done.

This was the end of my involvement with the situation."

* * *

Though there was no longer enough light for Eddie to read his watch, he guessed it was around 7:30 or so. The waves of panic had subsided a little, but they recurred every time he allowed himself to feel anxious instead of using his mind to figure out where he was. *I must be near a road, it's just too dark to see. All I did was ski the fall line down the mountain, how could I have gotten lost? Why were there no signs? Why was there no traverse leading back to the base? Shit. Don't think about that now Eddie. You're lost and it's freezing out here. Okay. I'm at the bottom of the mountain, there's got to be a road near here. I'll try 911 again, maybe they can guide me to the road.*

He doubted he would be able to get a cell phone signal now, as he was all the way at the bottom of this canyon. But he tried it anyway, and was surprised to find when he turned it on that there was one bar! His heart fluttered as he pressed the numbers 9,1, and 1. After two rings the operator answered. "911, where is your emergency?" It was a man's voice.

Eddie felt his body relax a bit as he spoke, he was so relieved to have reached someone. "I'm lost," he said simply.

"Hello?" said the operator.

"I'm lost," Eddie repeated.

"You're lost?" The operator seemed to be having trouble hearing him.

"Yes," Eddie replied.

The operator said, "Okay, um, do you know where you are right now?"

I just said I'm lost. Doesn't that mean I don't know where I am?

"Are you in Driggs or Victor?" asked the man.

"I'm in," Eddie began, and then corrected himself, "I was at Grand Targhee."

"You were at Grand Targhee?" the operator repeated.

"Yes."

"Were you skiing today?"

"Yes I was."

"Okay, and are you out in the backcountry or in the woods now?" the operator asked.

"Yes I am," Eddie said. He could faintly hear the tap tapping of a keyboard typing in the background.

"Okay, what was, do you remember the lift that you were on last, or which run you were?"

Eddie hesitated. "I'm far away from that though," he said.

"I'm sorry?"

"It was a double, double chair."

"You were on the double chair?"

"Yes," said Eddie decisively. "But I'm far out of the resort now, I believe."

"Okay... can you describe what kind, what area you're in right now?"

"Yeah, there's a meadow, there's a meadow here, there's a bunch of, uh, bunch of fallen trees it seems, there's a stream."

"There's aspen trees, you said?"

Eddie frowned. "I don't know what kind of trees they are."

"Okay. Do you have a GPS locator on you?"

"I do."

"You do?" asked the operator, surprised.

"Yes."

"Okay. Alright. And what's your name sir?"

"Fitzgerald."

"Okay..." Eddie heard the sound of typing. "Okay, what's your first name sir?

"I'm gonna run out, run out of juice, so, uh, Edward."

"Edward?"

"Yes."

"Okay. And what's the, what's the phone number you're calling me from?"

Eddie knew his phone was going to die any moment. "6314840313" he said quickly. "Slow down just a little bit—631?"

Eddie repeated the number a bit slower. He was sure it was important they have the number, even though his phone was going to die. But wouldn't the phone number come on the screen in the 911 office automatically? He knew in New York it would.

"0313. Okay," said the operator.

"Yes."

"Okay. Are you, are you, uh, do you have a room at Grand Targhee? Are you a guest there?"

"No I'm not," said Eddie. "I'm staying at the Parkway Inn in Jackson and all my friends are there." There was silence at the other end. He looked at his phone's screen—it was black.

In the dispatch office, Mark said "Oh, shit." He had lost the caller. He knew that Idaho did not yet have the capability of retrieving the location of a call. And his computer screen displayed only the last seven digits with no area code—but at least he had gotten the MP's area code just before they were disconnected.

Mark put down his earphone and mic headset, got up from his seat at the computer console and walked across the hall to the training room. The door was slightly ajar. He saw Terry Diamond talking to the new SAR recruits. Terry was facing in Mark's direction so Mark waved to get his attention. Terry gave him a questioning glance.

"What's up?"

"We may have a search," Mark said. The entire room of new recruits turned to look at him.

"Talk to me," Terry said.

"A skier just called, he's lost in the woods near Targhee. He says he was on the double chairlift, now he's in a meadow with fallen trees, or aspen trees, he said. He said he's got a GPS. I have to get back to dispatch, just wanted to give you a heads up." Mark quickly returned to the dispatch room.

"Hey Terry," said Dan Van Horst, a veteran Search and Rescue volunteer who was helping Terry run the meeting. The recruits were riveted on Terry and Dan now.

"I can go down to the Emergency Services Building and load the snowmobiles on the trailer, if there's going to be a search."

"That would be great Dan," replied Terry. "But let me see what's going on first. If I need you to do that, I'll give you the high sign. Can you take over the meeting while I deal with this?"

"No problem," said Dan.

Terry stepped out into the hallway, using his cellphone to retrieve the avalanche report from Bridger-Teton National Forest. The report came back "low at low elevations." Just as Terry entered the dispatch room to talk to Mark, the 911 line rang again and Mark quickly answered.

"911, where is your emerg—"

"I just called," Eddie interrupted.

"This is—Is this Edward?"

"Yes."

"Okay. Alright, Edward, hold on just one second, we're gonna get in touch with our people, okay?"

"Okay."

Mark Silver was using an earpiece and mic so Terry wasn't able to hear the caller. He would get the info from Mark later; in the meantime he stayed in the hallway and dialed Jackson Law Enforcement dispatch with his cellphone. "Hi Janice, this is Terry Diamond with Teton Search and Rescue in Driggs."

In the dispatch room, Mark was saying "I'm gonna keep you on the line... uh, do you see any lights at all?"

In the hallway, Terry said "We were having a little meeting right outside our, over here, and dispatch just grabbed me because we got a—"

Terry could hear that Mark was again speaking to the lost skier. He wanted Mark to get the skier's GPS coordinates. He held the phone away from his face and called out, "Just get the numbers." He put the phone back to his ear to continue the conversation with Jackson dispatch: "We got somebody that's been calling 911. They've skied out-of-bounds at Grand Targhee and found themselves in a field surrounded by trees. They're not sure where they are at."

Mark closed his eyes and his face puckered as he strained to make out the caller's speech coming through the headset.

"I'm gonna run out of juice though!" Eddie said emphatically.

"I'm sorry?"

"I'm gonna run out, run out of, uh, battery power," Eddie said, forcing himself to speak more slowly.

"Okay." Mark began typing in the information to the computer. "Now, are you a guest at Targhee, or are you just there for the day?"

"I'm, I'm not a guest there," said Eddie. "I'm, I was just there for the day." *Why was this guy asking all these stupid, irrelevant questions? I said I'm lost, he says 'do you know where you are.' And what difference does it make if I'm a guest at Targhee?* "I'm staying at the Parkway Inn," he said. He heard no response.

"Do you have your GPS out right now?" asked Mark. A vacuous silence answered him. "Shit," he said again.

In the hallway, Terry said to Jackson dispatch, "We are getting the information. But I'm just kind of giving you a heads up."

"I keep losing him," Mark called to Terry. "If I get the GPS coordinates from him can you talk him out of there?" He neglected to mention to Terry that the caller had said his cellphone was running out of battery power. He had heard Eddie say it, but it hadn't registered in his mind as important information.

"Yeah, no worries. You can just read the numbers off," Terry yelled back. If the caller could read off the GPS coordinates from his phone, they would know exactly where he was.

Terry returned to his conversation with Jackson dispatch. "It is in your jurisdiction... He is intermittent on his 911 calls when he calls in ... I do have somebody that is very familiar with the area. We were having a little get-together, our meeting, and he used to work up there for years and is very familiar, so we are hoping to, when he calls back, to put the two of them online and figure out where out-of-bounds he went, just to kind of help out ... yeah, I just didn't know if you wanted to let Don Oscar know and get them kind of under it. Sounds like this was something, sounds like something if we get all the right information it might be fairly easy to pluck him out of there ... all right, thank you, goodbye."

In the dispatch office, the 911 line signaled once more.

"911, where is your emergency?"

"This is Edward. Do you know where I am?"

"Uh, Edward—"

"Yes."

"I need you to tell me what kind of GPS unit you have," said Mark. "Do you know, is it one that gives you latitude-longitude, or is it a beacon, or is it a UTM…"

"It measures latitude, I don't know."

"It's latitude longitude?"

Eddie hadn't the faintest idea how the GPS on his phone worked, but 'latitude-longitude' sounded right. "Yes," he said.

"Okay. Do you have it turned on right now?"

"I don't know how it works."

"You don't know how it works? Okay. Do you, do you have it out right now?"

"It's on my cellphone. And I'm gonna run out of juice, so… hello?" Eddie looked at his phone. The screen was black. He pressed the power button. It would not come back on. That was it, his phone was dead.

Why was he asking me all those stupid questions? I shouldn't have told him I had a GPS, I don't even know how it works. And it's on my phone so it wouldn't have worked anyway. Shit. Well, they must've been able to trace my location by now, I called them three times. He put his phone back in his pocket and zipped his jacket up higher. He had felt warm enough while he was hiking down the mountain, but now that he had stopped he was starting to feel chilled. *Maybe they had time to tell where I am, can't they trace where the call was coming from? And Fred had to notice I'm not there, I wasn't on the bus. And Mario, and Larry, and Rich and Cheryl, they'll know I'm not there so I must be lost or in trouble, and they'll call the resort, and the ski patrol will come out and look for me. I'm just gonna wait right here by this stream. They'll probably be here in, like, an hour.*

Mark put down the headset and turned to Terry. "Lost him again. But now he says he doesn't know how to use the GPS."

"Listen," said Terry, "I have to get back to the meeting. When the guy calls back, just yell for me across the hall and I'll come back in and I'll help you talk him through it."

"Okay," Mark said. He looked over the notes he had entered in the log: the caller had said he was at Grand Targhee before he got lost. The calls had been interrupted before Mark could ascertain whether Edward was a guest at Grand Targhee, so he decided to call the Grand Targhee reception desk.

As Terry left the dispatch room, he dialed Jackson again to get Don Oscar's number. The dispatcher said she would ask Don Oscar to phone him back at the Idaho Sheriff's office.

Terry was never thrilled to talk to Don Oscar, who as Search and Rescue coordinator for Teton County Wyoming was Terry's counterpart—except that Oscar got paid, to the tune of 52 grand a year, and Terry Diamond didn't. Terry sometimes ran into Don at community functions. He was taller than Don, but found the short, balding man's commanding attitude somewhat intimidating. Terry thought of himself as a friendly person. He found Don Oscar to be rather snooty. Just because Oscar got paid for his position at Search and Rescue and Terry didn't, was no reason for being uppity. After all, they were both just trying to help people in trouble. Wyoming people in general, though, tended to act a little snooty towards the Idaho side of the county.

The economic disparities between the two Teton Counties did indeed create tension. Teton County Wyoming had one of the highest per-capita income levels in the United States. Teton County Idaho did not. Teton County Wyoming was the location of properties owned by celebrities and wealthy politicians. Teton County Idaho was not. Teton County Wyoming had a hot-shot Search and Rescue team that performed over sixty operations per year; Teton County Idaho's rescues could be counted on two hands. This dichotomy created a certain hierarchy, whereby Idaho often deferred to Wyoming as the leader of the pack. Thus when Terry Diamond found out there was a lost skier in Wyoming's territory, he didn't assume command of the incident. It was customary for him to just offer to "help out," because the Grand Targhee Resort was in Wyoming. This was Wyoming's baby.

Oscar called Terry back almost immediately, on the Idaho Sheriff's office landline. "Terry. It's Don. Dispatch said you called. What's happening?"

"Yeah, Don, thanks for calling back. Listen, Don, we have an incident in your jurisdiction. There's a lost skier who was skiing at Targhee, he said he's currently in a field with trees, he has a GPS unit but, I don't know, apparently, uh, he doesn't know how to use it, so..."

Don replied, "Did you get any more information from this guy?"

"Not really. We're waiting for him to call back. He called a few times but he, uh, he keeps getting disconnected. He's in Wyoming—or he was—but the calls are coming into Driggs, so ..."

Don always felt a little impatient with Terry Diamond. Terry tended to ramble, for one thing. And his team, Idaho SAR, was such a ragtag bunch. Clay Striver had tried to train them, but it was like pulling teeth to get those redneck yahoos to follow instructions. You'd be trying to assemble a hasty team and one of them would all of a sudden jump on a snowmobile and take off up the mountain, like he was Indiana Jones or something. That wasn't the way they did things in Wyoming. No sirree Bob.

Ed Fitzgerald Sr.: "He told them he was 'in a meadow' by a stream, with fallen trees. The 911 call detail report indicated that the transmission 'in a meadow' was received and understood ... Eddie was intentionally describing his location as 'in a meadow' because it was just that: a boggy area with a stream running throughout."

"We have one of our guys, he's very familiar with Targhee," Terry continued. "We were having our meeting right across the hall, so he, when the skier calls back, I can put the two of them on the phone and maybe figure out where the guy is at."

"Okay, that sounds good," Don said. "Keep me informed of what's going on."

Terry thought Don's tone was a bit terse, as usual. He never even had the courtesy to say "please."

"Okay good," Terry said. We'll keep you posted. Thanks Don." Terry hung up the phone, then picked it up again to dial the Grand Targhee main switchboard.

"Grand Targhee Resort, Katrina speaking."

"Hi Katrina, this is Terry Diamond from Teton County Idaho Search and Rescue, how you doing?"

"Oh, fine, Terry. What can I do for you?"

"Listen, could you possibly, uh, connect me with ski patrol? We've got a lost skier from Grand Targhee who's been calling 911 and it's bouncing over to our dispatch."

"Oh, okay," Katrina said, "Let my try to connect you ... but I don't think anyone's in the office now. It's after hours."

"Right, I realize that. I'll just hold on... or do you want me to call you back?"

"I'm pretty sure they've all left for the day, but let me try them."

"Okay thanks," said Terry. While he waited, he twirled the phone cord of the landline.

"I'm buzzing them now," said Katrina. "There's no answer and it's a pretty small room, so..."

Terry looked up at the clock—it was almost 8. "Well, thanks for trying, Katrina. Don't worry about it. I'll try reaching Jesse O'Leary at home. Bye, now." He hung up the landline and took his cellphone out of his jacket pocket. He had Jesse's number programmed into speed-dial but got his voicemail. He left a message. Now what? Well, Ned Schuman might be around, he's a Targhee senior ski patrol member as well as Idaho SAR, he would be good to get involved in this, Terry thought. He dialed Schuman's cell phone.

"Schuman."

"Ned, it's Terry. Can you talk?" Terry knew that Ned might be on shift, as the captain (and a paramedic) of the Teton County Fire Department.

"Sure, what's up Terry?"

"Well, we were having a Search and Rescue meeting over at the Sheriff's office and there's a skier been calling into 911. He said he'd been on the double chairlift at Targhee but now he's lost. The dispatcher says the calls keep getting cut off, and, uh, the speech isn't totally clear."

"Did he give any description of his surroundings?"

"He said there were aspen trees, uh, that's about it." The two men discussed the surroundings at Targhee for a few minutes, eliminating certain areas as being unlikely spots for the skier to have ended up.

"Well, it sure sounds to me like Rick's Basin, if there's aspen trees," commented Ned, "and if he was on the two-seater chair he could easily have ended up in there, in that Nordic area. Sounds like Jesse should be involved in this, since he's ski patrol *and* Idaho SAR. Did you call him yet?"

"I did, but he's not, uh, he didn't pick up, I left a message."

"Well, I'm on duty so I can't get over there. But if there's going to be a search I can help you guys mobilize from here, assist with the equipment. Oh, and you might want to get the head of lift maintenance over at Targhee in on this as well."

"Thanks Ned, that sounds good. Hey, I don't have Pete Kerry's number, um, or anyone else's number up there at Targhee, so ..."

"Okay, I'll make some calls. I'll get back to you."

"Thanks Ned, okay, bye."

When Ned got off the phone with Terry, he immediately called Jon Alexander, who was Acting Ski Patrol Director while Director Pete Kerry was out of town. He called Jon at home and on his cell, but had to leave messages at each one. Attempting to get ahold of someone in person, Ned called Jesse O'Leary next. Jesse was a senior ski patroller at Targhee, and head of the K9 avalanche unit as well. He would be the next in line as far as a leadership position. Although Jesse hadn't picked up when Terry had called him, Ned was able to reach him on the first ring.

From his location at the Fire Department, on Airport Road in Driggs, Ned gave Jesse all the information he had gotten from Terry Diamond: A skier from Targhee had been calling into 911 in Driggs while Idaho SAR was having their meeting right across the hall. The skier said he'd been on the two-seater chairlift (the Blackfoot lift) and was now lost. He was in an area with aspen trees, which Ned had determined could very likely be Rick's Basin, a Nordic ski area at Targhee. Just as Ned and Jesse hung up, Jon Alexander called Ned back. Ned gave Jon all the information as well, and made special note that the skier's calls had been repeatedly cut off, and that some of his speech had been unintelligible to the dispatcher.

Ned Schuman: "[Jon] began preparing to call patrollers to head back up to the resort and begin their search... I called Terry Diamond back informing him Jon would be the person in charge and that Jon would likely be calling him. After that I asked Terry if there was anything I could do from the Fire Department to help. That night I monitored the radio traffic and assisted SAR in the mobilization of vehicles and equipment. Other than helping establish communications and coordinate information between resort personnel and SAR, my activities [and] role centered around supporting from the valley floor while on shift at the Fire Department."

Jon Alexander: "I was at home around 8:30 in the evening when Ned Schuman called informing me of a 911 call about a lost skier at Targhee. I called Jesse O'Leary to confirm and talk about going up to the hill. I decided to get some patrollers to go see if we could determine where he went or if he was still at Grand Targhee. I called Andrew Iaukea to see if he was available. He was, and so was Jared Stanloff and Mandy Jones. Jesse came and picked me up and we met the other three patrollers at Targhee. Jesse was our liaison with Idaho Search & Rescue and Wyoming SAR. With the small info we had we decided to look below our Blackfoot area and in Rick's Basin."

The children's game "Telephone" starts with someone whispering a phrase to the next person in the circle, and so on, until the last person to hear the phrase repeats it aloud. The merriment ensues when comparing the final phrase to the original one. In Eddie "Cola" Fitzgerald's case, the telephone game had tragic results. On the phone with 911 dispatcher Mark Silver, Eddie said he was in a meadow with fallen trees. He never mentioned aspen trees, yet this description is the one that took hold in the minds and even the written notes of the search teams. Nobody from Search and Rescue, or Ski Patrol, listened personally to the recorded call. They were depending on the information conveyed to them by dispatcher Mark Silver. Besides "fallen trees," Eddie gave another important clue when he told Mark Silver he was near a stream. There is only one stream in the area, Leigh Creek. Had Mark Silver told the searchers that the lost skier was near a stream, they would have known immediately where he was and would not have wasted time searching Rick's Basin or the other areas of Targhee.

Terry Diamond: "I don't remember anything about a stream. I didn't learn of the stream until I think it was the next day when they were replaying that, that somebody told me about it."

Terry Diamond had been right there at the Driggs Idaho Sheriff's Office during Eddie's calls. He assumed Mark Silver had told him everything Eddie said. Still, since Eddie had originated from Grand Targhee, this was technically a Wyoming search and not an Idaho search. Therefore, Don Oscar from Wyoming Search and Rescue would be the one in charge, and Terry was just "helping out." Even though he felt his team could do the job, he would typically defer to Wyoming's authority. Terry did not like conflict.

Just as Terry found Don Oscar's attitude annoying, so did others—including Oscar's boss, Sheriff Jennings, and the Director of Wyoming Search and Rescue, Tom Catalin. Nevertheless, Oscar was the Wyoming SAR Coordinator, and a primary decision-maker in any incident. Don Oscar wasn't totally friendless, though. He was very close to Clay Striver, one of the most highly-regarded SAR experts in the area. Striver got along just fine with Don Oscar, and so did Len Jameson, the helicopter pilot. In fact, the three of them spent a fair amount of time together. When Don Oscar hung up the phone after speaking with Terry, his first thought was to call Clay Striver.

Fit, experienced, and intimately familiar with the Teton County wilderness areas, Clay Striver was considered an elder statesman and mentor by the Search and Rescue community. 61 years old, he was usually seen in a baseball cap that seemed to accentuate his angular features and trim white mustache and beard. He had "participated in over 900 missions and saved countless lives," according to the Teton County SAR website.

Striver had been buried in an avalanche as a young man, and was dug out by a Search and Rescue team. The memory of that incident had stayed with him. He began reading about the history of Search and Rescue, and was especially moved by the fact the majority of Search and Rescue personnel nationwide are volunteers. These volunteers often are led by paid personnel in law enforcement, the National Park Service, or branches of the military. He was thus inspired to become a Search and Rescue volunteer himself.

In addition to the standard Search and Rescue protocols, Striver also trained dogs used in avalanche rescues, as did Jesse O'Leary. The two men often trained their dogs together. No one would dispute that Striver's search and rescue credentials were top notch.

Striver's college Associates Degree was in Environmental Engineering, after which he joined the Army Reserves during the Vietnam era. His day job with Teton County was in the Planning Dept. From 1996 through 2010, with a few years off in the middle, he'd been the Training Officer for Wyoming SAR. He was also a former member, and Training Director, of Idaho SAR. As such, he was familiar with the scenarios that the Idaho SAR team had practiced. These scenarios included night searches. They also included searching South Leigh Canyon by going up from the bottom via snowmobile.

Striver held certifications in a wide variety of rescue operations including helicopter ops, rope rescue, swift water rescue, cave rescue, avalanche rescue and MLPI (Managing Lost Person Incident), and he trained Search and Rescue teams in these on a regular basis. When he taught the MLPI course, he instructed students in gathering information on the subject, determining the level of urgency, the mechanics of a search, the initial response period ("hasty search"), and other vital elements of the search process. In 1991, he himself was buried in an avalanche while backcountry skiing in Grand Teton Park with his two sons and their friend. They were able to rescue themselves without the aid of a SAR team. *Tom Catalin, WY SAR board member: "If I were lost, I would want Clay Striver looking for me."*

Don Oscar stretched out on his sofa, put one foot up on the coffee table, and took out his brand new iPhone to dial Clay's number. "Clay, it's Don," Oscar spoke into Striver's voicemail.

"Listen, there's an incident over at Targhee, a lost skier's been calling 911 and it's coming into Driggs dispatch. I just spoke with Terry Diamond, they were having a meeting over there and he's waiting for the skier to call back. He said he'd put one of his guys on the line with him and see if they can talk him out. Give me a ring back when you get this message. Thanks." Don then dialed Clay at his house, leaving a similar message.

Oscar was thinking that it was already after dark, and it was highly doubtful that the MP would be found via a ground search. So his next call was to Len Jameson, the helicopter pilot, to give him the heads up they might be needing him in the morning.

Even though Oscar was certain they would end up finding the MP in the morning via helicopter, since Targhee Ski Patrol was conducting a search of their grounds he thought it would be prudent to have a representative from the Wyoming team there. Clay Striver would be perfect for that job.

Oscar settled back on the sofa to watch television. He kept his cellphone nearby to catch Clay's return call. When Clay called back, he could pass this whole thing off to him. Even though, thought Oscar, the odds of finding a lost skier at night via a ground search weren't at all promising. Definitely, he thought, the most likely scenario was that the three of them—Oscar, Clay, and Len Jameson, would wait till morning, shoot up there in the heli, and grab the guy.

Don Oscar: "Clay Striver called back, I informed him of what I knew and asked him to work with the Driggs SAR team and to give Terry Diamond a call. I asked Clay to keep me informed. I called dispatch, and informed dispatch that Clay Striver was working with the Driggs team and that until we had more info which we were expecting to get when the missing person called back, there wasn't much more we could do at this point."

Oscar assumed that the lost skier would call back because Terry Diamond had said as much. 911 dispatcher Mark Silver, however, had not made note of Eddie Cola saying his cellphone was running out of power. Silver later said he didn't even remember hearing it. Thus, valuable time was lost as Terry Diamond and Don Oscar both assumed the lost skier would call back with a more detailed description of his whereabouts.

One wonders, however, what further description Eddie Cola could have provided. It was already after sunset when he was finally able to reach 911 for the first time, at 7:30 p.m. And in fact, he had already given Mark Silver the most important clue of all—that he was "near a stream." The stream was a vital piece of information, but Mark Silver did not convey it to the search teams. Eddie had said his cellphone was running low, and that he was near a stream. Silver later testified that at the time, he had not understood either statement.

When Oscar and Striver discussed the situation over the phone, their first thought had not been to page out the Wyoming SAR team. (All SAR personnel are equipped with pagers or other devices to receive text messages alerting them that a mission is beginning, and asking them to report for duty if they are available.) Instead, their first thought was to wait till morning and conduct the search via helicopter.

Oscar and Striver were both of the opinion that the helicopter was often the most efficient tool to use in a wilderness search. From the air, it was possible to cover a larger area in far less time, with fewer searchers. The only problem was that, for safety reasons, the helicopter could only be flown during daylight hours.

Oscar had spearheaded the funding drive to acquire a new building for Teton County Wyoming Search and Rescue, which would include a helicopter hangar, storage for equipment, and a training area. They were to break ground on the new building in the Spring of 2010. This would eliminate the need for housing the helicopter at the Jackson Hole Airport, where it was not as readily accessible for emergency missions.

In January 2010, Teton County Wyoming was leasing the helicopter services—a Bell 407 airship and pilot— from Hillsboro Aviation. The cost to the county was $27,000 per month for the winter season: December, January, February and Marcoh. Every hour of flight time cost an additional $1,600. Training sessions were billed at $1,200 per hour of flight time.

Naturally, every rescue accomplished via helicopter would further validate not only the fund drive for the new facility, but also the leasing and flight time fees paid by the county, totaling at least $30,000 per month.

Don Oscar wouldn't have admitted it even to himself, but he was hoping the lost skier would not be found that night and they would be able to use the helicopter. Heli missions always got his adrenalin pumping, and it sure beat sitting in the office shuffling papers.

Oscar was well aware that he would never be a contender in any Teton County Popularity Contest. But he didn't care. Rather than the superficial friendship of colleagues and acquaintances, he preferred the camaraderie of close buddies with whom he performed helicopter missions: Clay Striver and pilot Len Jameson.

Jameson lived near Striver, in Victor, Idaho. (When Oscar would move to Victor the following year, he would be neighbors with both Jameson and Striver.) Jameson's bio on the Hillsboro Aviation website noted that he attended pilot training in the U.S. Army in 1973. He flew UH-1Bs, UH-1Hs and OH-58 Scouts. In 1979, he started flying commercial operations, including seismic, fire fighting and utility work. In 1985, Len and his wife started their own company which grew to include five helicopters. Jameson served as the Chief Pilot, Director of Operations and part owner for 13 years. He then worked primarily in aerial fire fighting, helicopter skiing, search and rescue for the Teton County Sheriff's Department and as a company safety officer. He had logged over 22,000 hours of pilot in command time of which 16,000 hours where flown in mountainous terrain. He won several awards for mountain rescue, including the Robert Trimble Memorial Mountain Pilot Award from Helicopter Association International and the Jackson Rotary for Community Service award. He also worked with actor Harrison Ford on helicopter training and mountain flying when Harrison became involved in aviation.

Though Jameson had thirty seven years experience in aviation, he was extremely safety-conscious and did not take unnecessary risks. He was well aware of the danger involved in helicopter flight, but improvements in technology and weather forecasting since his early days of flying had reduced many of the risks that had plagued air travel in the past.

One of the earliest Search and Rescue missions in the Teton Mountain Range took place in 1950 on the days surrounding Thanksgiving, when a DC-3 plane crashed into Mount Moran. On board were twenty missionaries from California en route to Billings, Montana for the first leg of a trip to South America. They had lost their first plane, "Tribesman," earlier that year when it crashed in Venezuela. With donations received after the crash, the New Tribes Mission bought a new plane.

Weather forecasting was still in its infancy in those days and the pilot didn't know they would be flying directly into a storm whose thick clouds would not only obscure the 12,600 foot peak of Mount Moran, but also cause the plane's electrical system to fail. The rangers of Grand Teton National Park had to abort two SAR missions because of the continuing storm, but on the third day they reached the wreckage of the Tribesman II. There were no survivors.

* * *

"Search and rescue is an extremely diverse field that involves more art than science. Determining what will and what will not work is often based upon the educated opinions of those involved and these opinions may vary greatly ... a single tool should not be expected to work perfectly for every job... Nothing is more dangerous in SAR than an individual who lacks an open mind and thinks that he or she possesses the only true way. There are as many ways to perform any particular search or rescue as there are opinions on which is best. Every search and/or rescue can be improved upon." —*Fundamentals of Search and Rescue, (the textbook for NASAR, the National Association for Search and Rescue) pp. 2-3*

Jesse O'Leary, lead ski patroller for Grand Targhee as well as Idaho Search and Rescue, wanted to consult with Clay Striver before jumping into his truck and heading up to Targhee for a search . He had spoken with Ned Schuman from the Fire Dept., who had told him that Clay was already aware of the situation. With the combined efforts of both the Wyoming and Idaho Search and Rescue teams, in addition to Targhee Ski Patrol, they would be able to cover more ground in less time.

"Page out your team, we'll meet in Driggs," said Jesse when he reached Striver on the phone.

"No, Jesse," replied Striver. "We're not going to page out."

Jesse paused. He wasn't expecting this. He felt a slight surge of anger at the response of his mentor. "Why not," he asked.

"We don't search at night. People survive a night out all the time."

Jesse cleared his throat. "Well, yeah. But I had the impression the MP is from out of town, he's not a local."

"The MP was dressed for alpine skiing," replied Striver evenly. "It's not that cold out. We can take the heli tomorrow and find him easily."

Jesse was flummoxed. He was trying to act cool, but was shocked that Clay was refusing to page out the Wyoming team.

"Well," he responded, "We've got five from ski patrol going up to search Rick's Basin."

"Fine."

Jesse hesitated. "So, we'll keep you posted after we search. Talk to you later." He hung up, shaking his head. "Honey, have you seen my headlamp?" he called to his wife.

"You left it in the laundry room. Why?"

"I have to go. We've got a search up at Targhee."

His wife walked into the room. "Be careful Jesse." she said. "I always worry when you do a night search."

"Yeah, of course." He hugged her briefly and picked up his gear bag. "Can you believe, I just called Clay and he refused to page out their team!"

"Really? That's odd. Why?"

"I don't know. He said 'we don't search at night.' I don't get it. When Clay was training director for us, for Idaho, we did night searches."

"Maybe only Idaho does night searches. But Clay isn't an official member of Idaho SAR anymore, is he?"

"No, he's with Wyoming SAR now."

"So now that he's with Wyoming, maybe Wyoming doesn't do them," his wife commented, following her husband into the laundry room.

Jesse laughed. "Yeah, right." He checked the batteries in his headlamp and put it in the bag with the rest of his gear. He kissed his wife and went out to start his truck, tossing the bag in the back seat. He planned to pick up Jon Alexander and they would meet the other three patrollers up at Targhee. Hopefully they would find this guy, although they sure didn't have much to go on. The only information they had was that he was on the Blackfoot lift, skied down and ended up in a meadow with aspen trees. It sounded like he could be in Rick's Basin, so they'd probably start the search from there.

Let's see, thought Jesse, *we've got five Targhee ski patrollers for this search—me, Jon, Mandy, Jared and Andrew. But one of them will have to sit dispatch. I guess Mandy. So that only leaves four people to search. Well, the Idaho team is paging out, so they'll provide some more boots on the ground. But the incident originated from Targhee. Targhee is Wyoming, damn it. So the Wyoming team really should be there. What the hell is wrong with Clay?*

Clay Striver: "Basically I felt that my role was ... to be someone where Driggs and Grand Targhee solicited input on what they were doing, and if I felt that they weren't doing enough, that I would say something."

* * *

"Incidents must be managed in a systematic and consistent manner so that SAR personnel always know what job they are to perform, who they work for, who may work for them, who is in charge, and where resources are located. Improper management or poor organization can lead to inefficiency, ineffectiveness, and unsafe conditions for the subject and/or SAR personnel."
—*Fundamentals of Search and Rescue, page 24.*

At 8:30 p.m. Mandy, Cathy, Jared and Andrew were having dinner at the common house in Driggs after working ski patrol at Targhee all day. Just as they were finishing their meal, Andrew's cellphone buzzed. He pushed his plate aside and reached into the pocket of his cargo pants to retrieve it. "It's Jon," he said to the other patrollers as he glanced at the screen, "wonder what's up."

The other three watched Andrew as he listened to Jon. "Yeah," he said finally, "let me check it out and I'll call you back" he said. "Hey guys," he said to his companions, "there's a missing person up at Targhee, skied off of Blackfoot and now is calling 911. Jon is heading up there with Jesse and he wants to know can two or three of us meet him there."

Jared immediately said "Sure, yeah. I'll go, no problem."

Cathy chimed in, "Me too, I'm in."

"I know I'm a rookie, but I'd like to help," said Mandy.

"You've never been on a search before, though, Mandy," said Andrew.

"Yeah, you don't really have any experience," Jared added.

Mandy felt herself turning a little red. "Well, I don't know the backcountry very well like you guys, but I do have medical training."

"Well..." said Andrew.

Mandy realized she was pushing herself on them, when clearly she wasn't needed. Jon had asked for two or three patrollers, so it was already covered.

"Okay," she said, "You three go, I'll clean up dinner." She began gathering the silverware and stacking the plates as the others were putting on their jackets. Andrew began to dial Jon's number to tell him three of them were on the way.

"Oh wait!" said Cathy suddenly. "I just remembered, I'm on shift as ambulance driver at the hospital tonight!"

"Oops," said Jared.

"If this turns into something," Cathy told the boys, "I'll need to drive the ambulance." She turned to Mandy. "Mandy, why don't you go up for me?"

"Sure," Mandy said. "Even if you don't need me to search, I could at least sit dispatch."

The boys nodded and Andrew dialed Jon back. "Hey Jon—me, Jared and Mandy can pretty much leave right now. Where do you want us to meet you ... the parking lot? OK, see you soon."

Cathy began gathering the plates. Andrew, Mandy and Jared left the Common House, got into Jared's truck and made a quick stop at Mandy's house so she could pick up her headlamp. They arrived at Targhee about twenty minutes later.

The night was clear; it had stopped snowing some time earlier, and the stars were visible. The parking lot was empty save for several cars belonging to staff members working that night. Jon and Jesse were waiting for the three young patrollers by Jesse's truck. "Let's go to the snow safety office," said Jon as they approached. The layer of packed snow crunched under their boots as they walked to the snow safety office, in the bottom of the main building at the base of the resort, next to the First Aid Room. When they arrived, they were met by the Night Security Officer Clark Praline. He had been working when Katrina had received the call from the Driggs Sheriff's Office at the front desk—so he was the second employee working at Targhee that night to become aware of the lost-skier incident. He had radioed the snowcat operators who were grooming that evening, and asked two of them to leave their post on the main mountain and drive out to Rick's Basin, which was a section of the cross-country skiing area, to check for tracks.

Standing in the snow safety office with their gear bags, the patrollers listened as Praline told them what his snowcat operators had reported.

"They found boot pack prints on the outer loop of the Nordic area."

"Okay, thanks Clark." said Jon, "We'll go there first. And here's what else we know. The missing party called 911 from his cellphone, it got routed over to Driggs. The signal wasn't good and they kept losing him, but he last reported riding a two-person chairlift, so that means he was on the Blackfoot lift. I figure he's somewhere in the north end of the resort. According to Driggs dispatch, he also reported being in an aspen meadow."

"Is it just you searching, or is SAR being paged out?" asked Clark.

"Idaho SAR is sending three people," said Jon. "Jesse will be our liaison with Idaho. They should be getting here shortly."

Jared nodded and looked at Andrew, who smiled and gave a thumbs up. They were both excited to be involved with a search. Back at the common house, they had made a big deal out of Mandy's lack of experience regarding a search, but the truth was, they weren't very experienced either.

Jon continued, "Jesse and I are going to take a couple of snowmachines out to Rick's and investigate. Mandy, you'll be sitting dispatch. Andrew, Jared, wait here for instructions, we'll radio back to you. Mandy, I need you to brief the Idaho people when they get here. You'll handle all the incoming phone calls and radio transmission. Write down where all the search members go, what time they leave and what time they get back here."

Mandy went to the file cabinet where the forms were kept and took out several sheets of paper, and seated herself at the desk in the corner to prepare the first sheet. Andrew sat down on the bench. Jared inspected the edges of his skis. Night Security Officer Clark Praline said, "Looks like you've got it under control here. I'm going back to start locking up. Radio me if you need me, okay?"

"Thank you Clark," said Mandy. She had gotten some additional info from Jon, including the name of the missing party, and was already writing the known facts on the dispatch sheet: A lost skier named Edward Fitzgerald had called 911 a few times, and was able to speak with Idaho dispatch briefly before being cut off each time. He had last ridden on a double chairlift and described being in "a meadow full of aspen trees." He was not a registered guest at Targhee. The phone number he had called from was a New York number.

"Okay," said Jon, "Jesse and I are taking snowmachines out to search Rick's Basin and the North Boundary. So we're Hasty Teams 1 and 2." (In SAR parlance, a "hasty team" is an initial response team comprised of well-trained searchers who can mobilize quickly. Their primary responsibility is to check the most likely areas where the subject might be.) "I'll radio back to you guys," said Jon, as he and Jesse walked out of the room, leaving the younger patrollers to stand by for further instructions.

* * *

Terry Diamond paced up and down the corridor at the Sheriff's office in Driggs. He was still waiting for the lost skier to call back. He had received permission from Don Oscar to assist in the search by taking the two Idaho SAR snowmobiles to Rick's Basin. He called Targhee and spoke with Mandy, confirming that he was sending three members of Idaho SAR with two snowmobiles to assist in the search.

Helping out the search teams from the Driggs, Idaho end were Ned Schuman and Captain Gill from the Fire Dept. Dan Van Horst had left the meeting for new SAR recruits and driven straight to the Emergency Services Building, where he pitched in with Ned and Captain Gill to attach the trailer to the truck. "Hey, thanks Ned," he said to Schuman. "This makes things faster."

"Glad to help. Listen, I'm monitoring the radio. If there's anything I can do on this end, just let me know."

"Great. Thanks." Dan hoisted himself into the driver's seat and waited for Jack Stills and his wife Bev to show up. Like Dan, Jack and Bev were members of the Idaho Search and Rescue team, and Terry Diamond, their Commander, had requested the three of them to report to Targhee to assist in the search for the lost skier.

Dan had a hand-held radio with him, and the truck also had a radio for official communications. He would use the radio to report to Terry Diamond throughout the night. While he was waiting for Jack and Bev he decided to check with Terry to see if there had been any updates. Terry said that they were waiting for the lost skier to call back, but in the meantime, he advised Dan to go with Jack and Bev and the snowmobiles to stage at Targhee. (The "Staging Area" is the location to which SAR personnel and equipment are assigned.)

Dan: "Our options would have been Teton Canyon, Targhee and South Leigh Canyon, which are geographically a decent ways away. With our limited resources, the three of us and two snowmobiles, we felt the best place for us to go would have been Targhee."

With Idaho's two snowmobiles and Targhee's two snowmobiles that Jon and Jesse were already using, that totaled four snowmobile searchers just for Grand Targhee, primarily the section called Rick's Basin. But Eddie had clearly said to Mark Silver that he was "in a meadow with fallen trees". There were no fallen trees in Rick's Basin, a cross-country skiing area. There were, however, plenty of aspen trees. By this time the lifts had been closed for five hours. Eddie had been outside, lost in the snow and cold, since that time. Since he began skiing that morning, he had been outside for ten hours thus far.

After about fifteen minutes the Stills showed up. They each tossed a gear bag in the back seat of the truck. Jack jumped in the back with the gear, and Bev rode shotgun. "How you guys doing?" said Dan, pulling out of the parking lot.

"Good," Jack said. He was a rather short, stocky man with not much hair left, and he wore old-fashioned-looking wire rimmed glasses. Jack was a mild-mannered man with an agreeable personality. He was an ex-New Yorker who had moved to Teton Valley in 2006, and had been inspired to join the Idaho Search and Rescue team because he had assisted in rescue operations during the events of 9-11.

His wife Bev was a plain-featured, no-nonsense woman. The two of them were avid mountain bikers and were in good shape. They each had several years experience with Search and Rescue.

"Do we have any information," Jack asked Dan as they drove out of the parking area and onto the main road.

"Not very much," Dan replied. "Just that there's a lost skier who called 911. Terry is up there waiting for the guy to call back. He told us to bring the snowmobiles up to Targhee. Apparently Jon Alexander from ski patrol, and Jesse, and some others I think, are already up there." They continued up the long, flat two-lane highway toward Wyoming, accompanied by the static and bursts of conversation from the radio traffic, and the squeaks and rattles of the trailer behind them.

* * *

This is crazy. How did this happen? I wish they would hurry up and get here, I'm really getting cold now. I should stay by this stream, I told them I was by a stream. But if I walk around a little I could stay warmer. Maybe there's a road a little further down. There's stars out—shit, I wish I had taken a navigation course or something. Well, a lot of good that would have done me at home in New York, where you can't see the stars hardly. If I only knew how to work the GPS... forget it, moot point, the phone's dead anyway. Well, they must be on their way here, I'll just hang out a while, do some exercises or something. Try to keep warm. He began to do some jumping jacks, then it occurred to him that he might be better off conserving his energy. Still, he was cold. He stamped his boots on the snow, trying to revive his feet, which were beginning to feel quite numb. *Shit, I hope I'm not getting frostbite. I don't want to lose any toes!*

* * *

Transcript Of Recorded Phone Conversation Between Jackson Dispatcher And Sheriff Jennings, Teton County Wyoming:

Sheriff Jennings: Hello, this is Jim.

Dispatcher: Hi Jim, it is Karen at Dispatch. How are you doing?

J: I'm doing fine. How are you?

D: I'm good. I'm calling to let you know about kind of a situation that we've got going on. I'm not sure exactly what's going to happen with it which is why I was waiting a little while to call you.

J: Okay.

D: There's a skier who has gone out-of-bounds over near Grand Targhee. It was originally called in to us from Driggs Search and Rescue because it came into their 911 center and Don has called them and they're still kind of working on it 'cause they are not sure exactly where he is so we've just got it at a search and rescue now, hopefully ski patrol will be able to handle it but I've also called Suzie and let her know.

J: Now did he call it in himself that he was up there or did somebody call in as a missing skier? Do you know?

D: He called in himself. He's been calling their 911.

J: Got it. So we know he's doing okay he just needs some help getting down.

D: Exactly. He said they are probably just going to talk him out when they get ahold of somebody who knows the area and can direct him.

J: Okay, all righty, well hopefully he'll be able to get down sometime tonight.

D: Yeah, I hope so too. Do you want us to give you a call when it's resolved or do you want us to wait and let you know in the morning?

J: If it goes badly, in other words, if he falls or something and gets hurt, then a phone call would be great. But if not, if he makes it down or whatever I'd just wait till the morning.

D: Okay, I'll put in the notes.

J: Thanks a lot.

D: Have a good night.

D: You too, bye bye.

D: Bye.

END OF CONVERSATION

* * *

At 8:45 p.m. in the 911 dispatch office in Driggs, Mark Silver figured the key would be finding the lost skier's hotel. He then hoped to locate someone who knew the skier, so the search teams could get a better description of him, some background information.

If the lost skier wasn't a guest at the Targhee Resort, he might be staying at one of the other hotels in town. Mark had tried the Super 8, the Bunk House, Pines, Mountain View Lodge, all negative. Best Western was closed. What if the skier was staying at a private home, with friends? Well, hopefully then they would be calling the Sheriff's office, either Wyoming or Idaho, if their friend doesn't show up, Mark thought.

He looked up as Terry poked his head through the door. "Our lost guy didn't call back yet?" said Terry.

"Nope."

"Keep me posted," Terry said as he walked back to the training room.

* * *

Fred woke to the obscenely loud ring of the room phone on the nightstand. He reached over to answer it. "Yeah?"

"Uncle Fred!" It was his nephew Freddie. Freddie and Fred were rooming together, but Fred hadn't seen his nephew since they arrived at the Parkway Inn with Mario, in the van. Fred groggily sat up. He suddenly realized how exhausted he must have been, to have fallen asleep with his ski clothes on. "What's going on?" he said to his nephew.

"We can't find Eddie Cola," Freddie said.

"Whaddaya mean?"

"Well, his roommate, I forgot his name, said Cola's skis aren't there. I looked all over for you, I didn't think you'd still be in the room."

Fred looked at the clock radio on the nightstand; it was a few minutes after 9 p.m. Fred shook his head. He couldn't believe he had fallen asleep—he hadn't even had dinner. "Who's his roommate," he said, talking more to himself than to Freddie. "J.R.," he answered himself. He addressed his nephew: "Where's J.R. right now?"

"Oh, is that his name? He's in the lobby here with everybody. Want me to get him?" Freddie asked.

"No. No, let me go see what's going on. Maybe he just went out to dinner. Eddie Cola, I mean."

"Some of us went out to that Mexican place, Cola wasn't there," replied Freddie. "And there's a bunch of other people here in the lobby that went to different places, and nobody's seen him."

"Stay in the lobby. I'll be right there," said Fred, hanging up. He had been sitting on the edge of the bed; he now got up, grabbed his room key from the nightstand and put it in his pocket. "Jesus," he muttered to himself.

He walked down the reddish carpeted hallway of the inn and heard animated conversation coming from the lobby. When he arrived he saw at least a dozen members of the ski group standing around. Mackenzie, the daughter of the Parkway Inn's owner Joanie, was behind the front desk. Ted was leaning over the counter talking on the hotel phone, with a concerned look on his face.

"Fred," said Kathryn Sherlock, one of the veteran members of the ski group. "A call just came in to the hotel. Ted is still talking to them," she said, motioning toward the front desk where Ted was now holding the phone with one hand and writing something on a pad of paper with the other. "They're asking if there's a missing guest, because some skier from Targhee's been calling Search and Rescue," she continued.

"We think it might be Eddie Cola," Freddie chimed in.

"Wait," Fred said, shaking his head. He was still a bit groggy. "Who is it that's calling the hotel? Who is Ted talking to over there?"

"I'm not sure," Kathryn replied, "I think it's Search and Rescue, or the Sheriff's office. Anyway, J.R. is Eddie's roommate so he just went up to the room to check again.

Fred was starting to come out of his stupor. Eddie missing? This was unbelievable!

"Did somebody check to see if he's in the sauna, or the pool?" he asked.

"I already did that," said Ross. "It's just some old fat guy in there, Cola's not there."

Fred wanted to call Eddie right then, but he didn't own a cellphone and didn't know Eddie's cell number. "Kathryn," he said, "you have Eddie's cell number, don't you?"

"Larry already called," she replied. "It just went straight to voicemail."

"Well, try again," said Fred testily.

Kathryn dialed Eddie, but got the same result—the generic Sprint voicemail message.

"Where's Larry?" asked Fred.

"He's coming, he just went to look outside to see if Eddie was out walking around, maybe."

"Look, let's work backwards. When was the last time someone saw him," asked Fred.

Marco replied, "I saw him this morning, we were all skiing together, me and Ross, Cheryl, Rich and Eddie Cola. Then we went in to lunch but he didn't come with us. We went back out after lunch but I didn't see Cola anymore, that whole day."

"Wasn't he on the bus coming back?" asked Fred.

"Was he on the bus?" Marco turned to address all the ski group people who were standing around. "Did anyone see Eddie on the bus? Coming back, I mean?"

There was a chorus of no's.

"That's just so weird," Ross said. "If someone's calling Search and Rescue it means they're lost, and Eddie "Cola" Fitzgerald *never* gets lost."

* * *

Dan Van Horst eased the truck and trailer with the two Idaho SAR snowmobiles into the Targhee parking lot. He and Bev climbed out of the front seats, and Dan opened the door to the rear for Jack because it had a tendency to stick. Dan then radioed in to Terry Diamond to let him know they had arrived at Targhee.

"Well, let's unload these babies," Dan said. He and Jack proceeded to remove the snowmachines from the trailer while Bev stood outside the truck and looked for her snow gloves, inside her gear bag on the back seat. When the snowmobiles were unloaded and everyone had their gear together, the group made its way across the snowy walkway to the tower building adjacent to the parking lot. Once inside, Bev headed to the ladies room while Dan and Jack went into the snow safety office down the hall on the lower level. The door to the office was ajar. Jared stood near the door playing with his iPhone.

He looked up. "Hey," he said.

Dan extended his hand. "Dan Van Horst, Idaho SAR," he said. "This is Jack, and we have one more from our team with us. We've got two snowmachines waiting outside." Andrew came into the office carrying a soda from the vending machine just as Bev arrived in the room, and hearing conversation, Mandy rose from her spot at the desk in the back and went out to greet the Idaho SAR members sent to assist in the search.

Introductions were made, and Mandy said "Let me brief you guys, Jon and Jesse should be back here any minute."

"Not necessary," said Dan. "I was actually in the room over at the Sheriff's office when dispatch came in and told us about it."

"Oh, so you have been briefed already?" Mandy asked.

"Yeah, basically," he responded.

Mandy nodded and told the Idaho team that Clark Praline, the night security man, had already sent two groomers to the parking lot to check for any New York plates, but none had been found. Hasty Team 1, comprised of Jon on a snowmobile, was searching part of the cross country ski area known as Rick's Basin. The groomers had reported seeing tracks coming into the cross country trail at the low end of Rick's Basin; they had not seen any tracks on Quakie Ridge, but Jon planned to search there.

Mandy paused. "I'm not sure why he wants to search there if there were no tracks, I guess he just wants to verify that."

"No," said Dan, "Didn't the MP say he was in an aspen meadow? Well, 'Quakie' is a local term for aspen, so it would make sense to search there."

"Oh, I understand," said Mandy, a bit embarrassed that she didn't know this fact. She assumed a more authoritative tone of voice. "Also, Jon said he did find snowboarder tracks that approached Rick's Basin from the north. Unfortunately, the tracks had been partially groomed over, and he wasn't able to follow them to the end."

Mandy also advised the Idaho team that Jesse, as Hasty Team 2, had taken his German Shepherd Mickey, an experienced search dog, on the sled to check out the North Boundary area.

Mandy: "He had his avalanche dog also on the sled... we have at Grand Targhee five avalanche dogs. They're owned by paid patrollers. They raise their own funds for their own training and all their vet and medical expenses and provisions needed. The dogs train on a daily basis within the resort and are there as service dogs. In the event of a search and rescue or an avalanche inbounds, these dogs would be called to service to search the area."

Everyone looked up when Jesse strode into the office with snow still caked on his boots. "Hi Idaho SAR, how's it going?" He reached out a gloved hand in greeting. He already knew Dan, Jack and Bev, being a member of Idaho SAR as well as a senior ski patroller at Targhee.

Jesse O'Leary: "I went out [at 9:35 p.m.], found two sets of tracks, a skier track and a snowboarder track at the North Boundary ... the indication was the tracks hiked up onto the Nordic track. A groomer had reported some footprints on the Nordic track, but they had groomed over them. We had went out to investigate, took a dog out, investigated that area, saw [it] appeared only one set of tracks was coming up out..."

"Okay," said Jesse. "I'm going to take Mickey out to Rick's now. I want to take a look at the tracks Jon found." He left the room as quickly as he had come.

Mandy Jones: "They both went to that location first because they had had from the snowcat drivers a report of footprints in the Nordic area, which is unusual. There wouldn't be anyone hiking out there. So they both responded there to try and clear that area and/or see if there were any other leading tracks or identifying marks... they found boot prints, but they were feeling based on the shape of them that it was a snowboarder. They weren't satisfied because of our description. We were told that Ed was a skier or on skis. So Jesse continued in this area."

There weren't enough chairs available in the office, so Bev and Jack sat on the hospital beds in the adjacent First Aid Room, while Dan paced back and forth in the small office. Jared and Andrew discussed a ski film they had both seen while Mandy looked up the sweep records in the Daily Summit Log. She found that Kris Hart had been assigned the sweep for the Blackfoot lift, which was the only two person chairlift at the resort. Kris had not noted seeing any tracks leaving the boundary. She decided to call him on his cellphone to ask him about it, and advise him about the lost skier.

The phone rang several times. Just as she was sure the call was going to go to voicemail, Kris finally picked up. "Hello?" he answered groggily.

"Hi Kris, it's Mandy from patrol. Sorry to bother you, but we have a search going on. We have a skier who's been calling 911, he said he skied off the Blackfoot lift and then got lost. I'm on dispatch, so I wanted to ask you, did you see any tracks leaving the North Boundary when you did your sweep?"

"Uh, I don't think so," he said in a muffled voice. Mandy wondered if he was completely awake. "Oh wait, wait a minute," he said. "I did see some tracks. They looked like snowboarder tracks though."

"Leaving the boundary?" asked Mandy.

"Yeah. I just figured it was a local."

"Okay. Thanks Kris."

"What's going on?" He sounded more awake now.

"I can't talk now. I have to brief the Idaho SAR people."

Mandy didn't much like Kris. On her first day as a patroller at Targhee, he had spoken to her rather condescendingly and she had resented it. As time went on, she noticed he was always the last to volunteer for anything, and the first to leave as soon as his shift was over. She was relieved to say goodbye.

Mandy wrote down in the dispatch report that Kris had seen snowboard tracks leaving the resort boundary. Suddenly the radio crackled, and she took the call from Jon. "There are three people here from Idaho Search and Rescue," Mandy said into the radio handset. "What do you want them to do?"

"Well, I think they should really be searching from the other side, down in South Leigh, in case the guy made it down that far."

"Do you want me to tell them to do that?" Mandy asked.

"Not yet. Jesse just got here with Mickey. We're going to inspect the tracks again. Tell them to stand by, and I'll get back to you." Jon signed off and Mandy wrote another note on the dispatch report.

* * *

"You guys, please shut up!" yelled Ted, covering the phone with his hand as he turned around to the ski group milling around in the lobby. "I can't hear, okay?" Ted turned his back to them once more, hunched over the front desk with a pen and pad of paper to write down the phone number of whoever he was supposed to call next. A fireman used to handling emergencies, Ted had taken it upon himself to be the ski group's liaison with Search and Rescue. *Fred is just about useless right now. He's acting like a basket case, with Mario breaking his leg and all,* he had thought. *I better do this myself. Christ, it's already 9:30 at night, I wish we had known about this earlier!*

Ted scribbled down Terry Diamond's phone number. "Okay, thanks, thanks a lot," said Ted into the phone. He turned to the ski group people who were waiting expectantly, glad that someone had taken charge of the situation. Some of the group didn't know Eddie well, but they were very concerned about him being missing.

"Do you think it's Eddie?" Kathryn asked.

"It could be," replied Ted. "There's a skier calling 911, and we can't find Eddie, so it could very well be him."

"Ted," said Fred, "Are you, like, taking care of this? I mean, you're going to keep in communication with the Search and Rescue people?"

"Of course," Ted replied. "Yeah, I'll do it." He glanced down at the piece of paper in his hand. "Listen, I'm going upstairs to my room, I'll use my cell phone to call these guys. If Eddie shows up someone let me know, okay?" Ted headed towards his room. Being in the lobby with all those people talking was too distracting. Once in his room he sat down at the desk with the piece of paper in front of him, and punched in the numbers on his cellphone. It was getting a consistent signal, at least in Jackson. Over at Grand Targhee it had been a different story. He'd heard several people in the group complain about the lack of cellular signal there. If anyone was expecting Eddie to call, they were dreaming.

* * *

Eddie Cola lifted his face from the snow. He wiped his eyes and realized his glasses were missing. "Damn!" he exclaimed loudly, though there was no one there to acknowledge that he had tripped on something—a tree root? A rock? He knew he was unhurt, just needed to stand up again. His glasses had flown off his face though. His ski goggles had held them in place on the mountain, but he had taken off the goggles while he hiked alongside the stream. As he stepped over fallen trees and carried his skis under his arm in the dim twilight, he found it difficult to keep his balance.

I told 911 I was in a meadow with fallen trees. But didn't I also tell them I was near a stream? Yes, I'm sure I did. Pretty sure. Didn't I? I can't think! What's wrong with me? Eddie scrunched his face up and opened and shut his eyes several times, as if to lubricate the synapses in his brain that didn't seem to be firing. *Well anyway, they should figure out I had to keep walking to stay warm. I'm still by the stream, even if I'm not in that meadow ... I'm still, by, the stream. I'm still, by, the stream ...*

Eddie turned his last thought into a sing-songy phrase that he hummed softly as he tried to get onto his knees. He was learning the guitar. His teacher had told him he should make up some songs of his own, and sing them while he accompanied himself. He hadn't made up any songs, because he hadn't been able to think of any. But now, as he was lost in the woods, in the dark and the biting cold, little melodies were coming into his head, all by themselves.

Eddie fell over again. He was extremely nearsighted. Without his glasses he felt very disoriented. *I need to find them.* He righted himself and stuffed his gloves into his jacket pocket. He proceeded to methodically reach out to a radius of two feet or so, gently brushing his hands over the snow while moving his body in a small circle. He went around and around over the same ground. Sometimes he reached a little further, in case they were just beyond the perimeter.

The moon was a waxing crescent, but its beams were stolen by boughs of Douglas Fir. Eddie squinted as he covered the search area, hoping that the moonlight, faint though it was, might lend a small glint to his glasses. From his first waking moment until going to bed for the night, he was never without them. He was now lost, freezing, and blind.

He suddenly realized he had been kneeling in the snow looking for his glasses for some time. *Shit! Now my pants are wet. Damn it! Maybe it's time to give up.* He raised his head. His impaired vision turned trees and snow mounds into only the vaguest of outlines. Eddie knew that in these dense woods, he needed at least one hand free if he was going to continue without glasses—he didn't want to get poked in the eye by a branch. *Time for an executive decision.*

Eddie wiped his hands on his jacket and put his gloves back on. He took his ski poles in his right hand and stood up. He brushed the snow off his pants. He knew the stream was to his right, he could hear it. He took one halting step, then another. His skis remained where he had left them, lying in the snow. They were no longer a priority. Eddie continued to inch along, left hand in front of him, right hand using his ski poles to balance himself. He was completely focused on forging his slow path through the woods. *I can't see shit. But I've got to keep moving. I'll stay close to the stream and it should lead me to the road.*

* * *

In the 19th century, explorers like John Colter and Meriwether Lewis hired Indian guides to help them navigate unfamiliar territory. Today in the 21st century, the equivalent of Indian guides are the locals—the men and women who grew up in the backcountry. They're the ones who, as children, played in the caves or the mountains or the woods. As adults, they continue their friendship with the land on skis, on snowmobiles, on watercraft and aircraft, and on foot. A "foreigner" sees the woods as a mishmash of random trees with fallen logs and a stream here and there. Locals, however, see neighborhoods— as did the former inhabitants of the lands, who gave names to those places: "Red Bank of a River"; "Place of Many Hills"; "Where the Valley Widens"; "Thick-Necked Giant"; "Where The Wild Potatoes Grow."

One might compare the wilderness environment to a kennel full of collies. All collies look like Lassie, unless one is a breeder of collies. Or a collie.

Sometimes snowmobilers will encounter cross-country skiers touring the same backcountry. The skiers give the snowmobilers dirty looks: the swoosh of skis harmonizes with the wind and the gurgling of the creek, but the snowmobile lunges Harley-Davidson-like through the quietness, sounding like a chainsaw and stinking of gasoline.

But when a skier or hiker becomes injured and is stranded, immobilized, in that wilderness, no sight is more welcome than that of a snowmobiler. For the "snowmo" boldly goes where no other vehicle has gone before. It does so over snow, over ice, up mountains and down again, occasionally forging virgin paths but usually following the Forest Service logging roads.

The winter slopes of South Leigh Canyon are a temptation a local expert snowmobiler can't resist. Sometimes a passenger will be on board as well, as the snowmo lurches over the crystallized path of the access road until it reaches smoother ground a little ways further up. But even then, if the road is packed down with ice, the unsuspecting passenger will need to hug the driver's waist as they lurch from side to side, sometimes narrowly escaping being tossed out into the arms of the ever-present Douglas Firs. Or if it has just snowed, and the powder is knee high, the riders will plane across the top in a swingy, loopy fashion that is even more unstable than the first scenario.

Either way, a newbie passenger is in for a hair-raising experience; but there is nothing for it but to settle down and relax, allowing one's weight to sink, and roll with the flow. Then one will gaze wonderingly at the passing landscape, a seemingly endless panorama of winter woods in picture-postcard perfection.

* * *

"The goal is to put a team in the right location as soon as possible."
—*Lost Person Behavior by Robert J. Koester, page 295.*

Jon radioed in and spoke with Mandy. "Can you tell Jared and Dan to gear up the snowmobiles and go from the base of Sac, check the cat ski area, Mill Creek, and check the southern boundary?"

She wrote down his request and relayed it to Jared and Dan who left immediately, anxious to contribute to the search. Andrew and Bev were still waiting for an assignment. "He didn't say anything for me to do?" asked Andrew.

"No, not yet. But he will," said Mandy.

The desk phone rang. Terry Diamond was on the line. "We just heard from a member of the missing person's ski group. I've got a profile, do you want to write it down?"

"Yes, please," responded Mandy, her pen poised.

"OK. This is from some guy named Ted Norton, his phone number is 516-930-5085. He's in Room 50 at the Parkway Hotel in Jackson. He gave me this description of the skier: Height is five-eight or five-ten. He had on a red jacket and black pants, and he wears glasses. He's a 46 year old male skier here with a ski club from Long Island, New York." He paused. "Have you got all that?"

"Hold on... yes, thanks," responded Mandy, writing quickly. "Anything else?"

"He's part of a group. They've got fifty four people. Uh, there was something, an incident earlier, one of their members took a fall and went to the hospital—"

"Yes," Mandy interrupted him, "I was working then. That's the gentleman who broke his tibia, or fibula. They sent him to the Emergency Room at Driggs. That was about 2 o'clock this afternoon. So, the MP was a member of this same ski group?"

"Right. This guy Ted said when they picked up the injured party from the hospital, everybody reorganized in their cars or whatever, and nobody noticed that the missing person wasn't there. Uh, let's see if I have any more information for you ... yeah. Ted says, no medical conditions, non-drinker, he's an introvert."

"Did you say 'introvert'?" asked Mandy.

"Right. You know, like someone who doesn't talk a lot ..."

"I know what an introvert is," said Mandy.

"Oh, okay, sorry. Um, also, he's apparently, according to Ted, not the type that would break the rules, you know, ski out of bounds. Ted said that the MP is ... uh... likely very scared, but he may not flag down someone he doesn't know."

"Okay," said Mandy slowly, still writing. "Thank you so much Terry, this is very helpful. I'll radio this in right away. Oh, I need to know how I can reach you."

Diamond gave her his number, as well as Don Oscar's number, and signed off. Mandy immediately radioed Jon out in the field.

"Jon, I have a description of the person who is probably the MP. Terry just got this to us. The MP's ski group leader called in because he's been missing." She conveyed the information she had been given.

"Do you have a phone number for the ski group leader?" asked Jon. She answered affirmatively. Jon's voice got fainter as he turned away from the radio, but Mandy could hear him asking Jesse to put the number in his cellphone.

"What's his name," Jon asked Mandy.

"Ted Naughton."

"Okay, I'll tell Jesse to call the ski group leader directly," Jon said. He signed off.

Mandy Jones: "Jon took it upon himself early in the night to call this individual [Ted Knowlton]... and speak with him to try and gain more access and information or insight to Ed's kind of personality and not just the logistics of what he was wearing, what he had with him ... provisions [if] he might have to spend the night in this environment. He wanted to know more about maybe Ed's intent. Was this individual suicidal? Was he out there ... because it was an accident ... we were trying to gain more information about how Ed ended up where he ended up. So in calling the tour group person ... we were informed that Ed was not a thrill seeker. That Ed wouldn't step six inches outside of a boundary rope to take a good picture. That he was very much by the book and by the rules. And that this person believed this was wholeheartedly an accident and Ed needed saving."

Mandy turned to Bev Stills, who with Andrew was still waiting patiently in the office for an assignment in the search. Bev had located a folding camp stool and had brought it over to sit next to Mandy.

"The MP has been out at least since the lifts closed at 4," Mandy said. "He's very possibly hypothermic by now."

"I'll bet you're right," replied Bev. "They need to find him fast. You said he was on that two-seater lift?"

"That's what was reported by 911 dispatch. But you know, sometimes people get confused about which lift they were on."

"Well," said Bev, "I think until we got this new information we were basically shooting in the dark. It's a good thing the group leader called in."

"Absolutely."

Andrew had been pacing anxiously around the tiny office for several minutes. "Mandy," he interjected, "Do you think I should gear up and go out to Rick's Basin and help them out? I'm just here doing nothing." He didn't know why Jon had asked for Jared to go out, instead of him. He was just as good a skier as Jared.

"No, Andrew, just wait. They have enough searchers there. They may need to send you somewhere else. Jon will call for you soon, I'm positive."

Mandy sometimes found herself mothering the boys a bit; she was a little older than they were. She didn't really mind, but their emotional immaturity was a bit irritating at times. Andrew went back to playing with his phone while Mandy and Bev continued to discuss the likelihood of the lost skier being hypothermic.

"Did anyone from your team actually listen to the 911 call?" asked Mandy. "Possibly they could detect from his voice whether he's showing signs of hypothermia, like slurred speech."

"We did not hear the playback," Bev said. "I assume Terry listened to it, but I don't know for sure."

"Hey, Mandy," called out Andrew, "Look at this." He brought his smartphone over to the desk, pointing at the screen. "This is so cool! Google maps shows the Targhee trails in the 'terrain' view," he said excitedly.

Bev and Mandy leaned over to look at the display.

"See, if he was skiing off Blackfoot and he crossed the North Boundary Traverse," said Andrew, pointing out the cleft that cut through the mountain ridge, "He'd be heading straight for the chute. That chute would be the fall line going down, so it would be his natural path of travel. I mean, it's possible he could have crossed into Rick's Basin, but only if he went in right here." Andrew indicated an opening into the basin on the map. "If he missed that opening, he would be here." He moved his finger up the screen. "From this point, he wouldn't be able to do anything but continue down the chute."

"What's that?" Mandy pointed at the blue line running perpendicular to the chute.

"That's South Leigh Creek," said Andrew.

"So if he went down that chute, he would end up by that creek?" Mandy asked.

Andrew switched the device to the "hybrid" view. "Well," he said, "the chute would dump him right here, in this meadow, see?" He pointed to a clearing amidst the dense trees, adjacent to the creek.

"This is interesting," said Bev as she looked over Mandy's shoulder at Andrew's smartphone. "I've never seen this before."

"Maybe you should show this to Jon and Jesse," Mandy said.

"Nah," said Andrew. "It's just a map. Those guys know this area like the back of their hand. They don't need maps." He switched off the display and put the phone in his pocket.

* * *

"For SAR personnel and the subjects of their toil, hypothermia should be considered the most potentially important outdoor danger that is likely to be encountered."
— *Fundamentals of Search and Rescue, page 118*

Deputy Dina Dammer had been enjoying a quiet evening in her log home in Victor, Idaho, when the call came in.

"Hi, Dina? It's Rick from the Sheriff's Office, how are you?"

"Hi Rick. I'm fine, just relaxing."

"Look, I'm sorry to have to ask you this, but could you report for duty? I'm by myself here and there's some incidents we're dealing with. The thing is, there's a lost skier who's been calling into Driggs dispatch, and we need someone to go to his hotel in Jackson to interview his ski group, and basically be the liaison from Idaho."

"Oh ... okay, sure, Rick." Dammer was tired, but she could not refuse a request to report for duty—it was part of the job. There was a pad of paper and a pen on the coffee table; she pulled these closer and said, "What's the hotel, and the address?" After receiving a briefing on the incident, she hung up and said, "Sorry, sweeties," to her two black, silky-coated cats as she tossed them gently off her lap. She went into the bedroom to remove her sweatpants, fleece vest and bunny slippers and put on her uniform again. It had been a long day but apparently it wasn't over.

Deputy Dammer's duties included responding to burglaries, domestic calls, car accidents and enforcement of traffic laws. She was also authorized to make arrests, investigate crime scenes, and respond to calls for service on an emergency or non-emergency basis. For some reason, this particular call gave her a bad feeling. She sometimes had premonitions, if that's what you'd call them. Like her mother, she was extremely sensitive to people's "vibes," and that stood her in good stead in the law enforcement business. Her sixth sense about people, what their motivations and intentions were, made her a valuable part of Sheriff Lichevy's Teton County Idaho team. He often relied on her for the difficult jobs that required good rapport with people. The present scenario fit that description perfectly, as the missing skier was evidently visiting from New York with a large group of his friends. Dammer would have to interview the ski group leader, and possibly other members of the group. But she had "that feeling" in her stomach. Whenever she had "that feeling," things usually didn't turn out so well.

"I'm sorry darlings," she told the felines in a soothing voice. "Here's some treats for you." The cats ate the tiny fish-shaped treats eagerly, and looked up for more. "Mommy will be home soon," Dammer said. She locked up and went out to the driveway. She opened the driver side door to her police cruiser. First she checked that the rifle was securely in its supports in the front cab. She also had a shotgun and a shell belt strapped in the back trunk space. The back seat was almost entirely taken up by the perp cage. She got in, fastened her seat belt and prepared to make the drive over the Teton Pass to Jackson. The dashboard clock read 9:10 p.m.

Frequently it would be snowing on the pass, even when it wasn't snowing in Jackson or Driggs. Such was the case this evening, and she slowly made her way to Jackson, putting her truck in low gear to descend the steeper grades and navigate the hairpin curves. It took the better part of an hour to make it over the pass.

When the Deputy arrived at the Parkway Inn in Jackson, Ted was still upstairs in his room. He had just gotten off the phone with the night auditor at Grand Targhee. "Has he been found?" Ted had asked the auditor hopefully. Receiving a reply in the negative, he sighed. The night auditor transferred Ted to the Targhee front desk, where he spoke with Katrina. He gave her the same description of Eddie that he had given Terry Diamond. He hung up and leaned back in the chair, putting his feet up on the desk. Things weren't looking good. At this point Eddie had been lost on the mountain for more than six hours apparently, because the lifts had closed at 3:30 or 4:00 and it was now well past 10 p.m. Ted looked up when someone knocked on the door of his room. He opened it and found a nervous and exhausted-looking Fred standing before him.

"Hey, Ted, there's a deputy here, from the Sheriff's office, downstairs," said Fred. "She wants to talk to us. Can you come down?"

"Yeah, sure." Ted went back to the desk to grab his cellphone and his room key, and followed Fred down the red-carpeted stairway. Deputy Dammer was standing in the lobby. She introduced herself to Ted, and invited the men to sit down with her in the lobby. Kathryn Sherlock, waiting downstairs, introduced herself to Dammer. She had been hanging around the lobby waiting for Eddie to show up ever since she heard he was missing. She was one of the group members, along with Fred, Larry and Mario, who was closest to Eddie. Her stomach felt queasy over Eddie being missing. Thank goodness this deputy had shown up. At least, it was an indication that there were people looking for him, and something was being done.

Dammer seated herself in one of the comfortable armchairs near the window, and took out her notebook and pen.

"Can you tell us anything?" asked Kathryn. "What's happening? Do they have any leads?"

"What I can tell you is that we have the best Search and Rescue people in the county looking for your friend," the deputy began. "The Commander of Idaho SAR, Terry Diamond, is right now at the Sheriff's office in Driggs. We're hoping that your friend will call us back with more information."

"When was his last call?" asked Ted.

"I believe around 7:30," said Dammer. "He made two or three calls apparently. He may have called back after that, but I'm not aware of it."

Fred remarked in a raspy voice, "None of the phones, I mean, nobody's phone is working too good here. Everybody's complaining that I don't have a cellphone, but people said the signal isn't too good."

Ted added, "Yeah, I tried to make a couple calls from Targhee and couldn't get through, so... I don't know if you guys should be waiting for him to call back."

Dammer nodded and said, "Tell me about this afternoon, when he was last seen."

"We don't know much," said Fred. "He was definitely on the bus going over, then I don't know because I didn't actually ski with him."

"Who could have been skiing with him," Ted said.

"Well, probably someone he knows, like, not one of these new people," Fred replied. "He's kind of shy meeting new people. It might have been somebody like Cheryl. Hey, has anyone seen Rich and Cheryl?"

Ted and Kathryn both shook their heads. Kathryn said, "I saw them getting off the bus when we arrived back here in the evening, but I don't know where they went after that."

"Tell me about that," said Dammer. "How come nobody noticed that Edward was not on the bus going back to Jackson?"

Fred described how Mario had broken his leg on the mountain, and that the seating on the buses had to be rearranged in order to accommodate him.

"Didn't anybody do a head count after everyone was seated?" asked Dammer.

Fred shook his head. "No. I should have, but, you know, it was just so confusing. Everyone was asking me questions, you know. People wanted to know whether everyone had to go to the hospital... people were switching buses—"

"So you didn't do a head count," said Dammer, writing it down in her notebook.

"No. There was too much happening." Fred turned slightly pale as a wave of anxiety pulsed through his body. He realized that not having taken an accurate head count had been a big mistake. He was afraid the deputy would start grilling him even more, and was relieved when Ted's cellphone rang.

"Let me take this," Ted said, walking into the breakfast room.

"Ted, it's Jesse from Ski Patrol. Is there any more information you could give us about Edward?"

"Well," said Ted, "it's basically what I already told you guys. I'm not sure what I could add to that."

"What was his job?" asked Jesse.

"He worked for the Postal Service."

"As what?"

"As a mail carrier."

"So he was in good shape, walking every day?"

"Yeah, definitely."

"Do you know if he skied with a day pack?"

Ted thought a moment. He had never seen Eddie with a knapsack, or anything like that. Eddie always wore the same thing to go skiing: black pants, black gloves, and that red Coolar jacket. "No, no day pack," said Ted. "But there's one other thing, actually. Eddie might be autistic."

"He might be autistic?" repeated Jesse. "Well what is his skiing ability then?"

"Oh, it doesn't affect his skiing. He's a pretty good skier. He functions pretty normally, I guess, but he doesn't talk much."

"So he didn't carry a day pack, he didn't have any backcountry gear," Jesse said.

"No, definitely not," said Ted. "And listen, if you guys are waiting for him to call back, it's probably not gonna happen because our cell service wasn't good on the mountain."

"Yeah, it's spotty all around here," Jesse agreed. "Okay, thank you for the information. We're continuing with the search."

"Thanks. Please let me know as soon as you've found him, okay?"

"We'll be in touch."

Ted closed his phone and put it back in his pocket. He returned to the lobby and related his conversation with Jesse to Deputy Dammer, Fred and Kathryn.

"To your knowledge," said Deputy Dammer, looking at Fred, "has Eddie ever participated in any programs where he learned survival type skills, like making shelter, making fires, those sorts of things?"

"No," said Fred. "Because when we camped out, we car camped. We would pull up to the camp site and then we would just unload the gear and we usually stayed in a lean-to, sometimes tents."

"So, as far as you know, he didn't really have any outdoor skills?"

"I don't think so," said Fred. "We just like, went hiking and did basic camping."

"Do you think Eddie could have skied out of bounds on purpose, you know, just to get to some powder?"

"Definitely not," said Fred emphatically. "Eddie didn't ever go out of bounds. Me neither. We don't go out of bounds."

Dammer closed her notebook and said "Okay, if Edward shows up here at the hotel, you must inform us immediately."

"Yes, of course," said Ted and Kathryn simultaneously. Fred nodded. "And you'll call us if you find him," he said. "I mean, when you find him, right?"

"Don't worry," Dammer assured him. "We have the best people looking for him." She said goodbye and got back in her cruiser. It was going to be a long night.

* * *

"Hey Sharon," said Mark as Sharon Courier, his relief, walked in the door to the dispatch room.

"Hi Mark. What's going on?" She sat down without taking off her coat and hat.

Mark briefed her as to the status of the search. "Oh," he continued, "we got a little new information also. The tour leader called in at 10:21. His name's Ted Nalton. He gave us a clothing description of the MP."

"Wow, so they've been searching since 9 or so, but they haven't found him?" Sharon asked.

"No, not yet. We're waiting for him to call back."

"How long has it been since he last called?"

"Well, it's 11 now, and he called last at 7:30. So it's about three-and-a-half hours."

"That's a long time. Do you really think he's going to call back?" said Sharon. "That doesn't seem too likely to me."

Mark reached for his coffee cup and took a swig. The coffee was cold but he didn't care, he was used to it. He actually kind of liked it. It made him feel like one of those detectives in the movies. Weren't they always drinking cold coffee? He scrolled through a couple of screen shots on the computer and glanced at the dispatch notes. "All I can tell you is, Terry Diamond is here. He's running the show, and he thinks the guy will call back."

Just then Diamond walked into the dispatch room.

Mark spun around in his chair to face Terry. "Speak of the devil, we were just talking about you Terry."

"Oh, hi," said Terry, seeing Sharon. He turned to Mark. "Just checking in. Did Edward call back yet?"

"No," said Mark.

Sharon noticed Terry looked tired. He had probably been working the entire day, and now he might be up for several more hours directing his Idaho Search and Rescue team.

"Terry," she said, "Mark just briefed me on the incident. "I'll be here all night, so whatever I can do to help."

"Thanks," said Terry.

Sharon stood up to take off her coat. "My glove!" she exclaimed suddenly, holding one glove in her hand and searching her coat pockets with the other. "Oh, I hope I didn't lose it, I've already lost one pair this winter."

"Maybe you dropped it outside," said Mark.

"I'll go look," said Sharon. She walked back out the front entrance and saw the glove lying in the snow just outside the door. *Thank goodness*, she thought, *I really didn't want to buy another pair of gloves.* She shook the snow off the glove as she walked down the hall to the dispatch room. As she approached the open door she heard Terry and Mark in conversation.

"I think anybody dumb enough to be out in this weather, unprepared, probably deserves to spend the night out there," Mark was saying.

"Doesn't matter how dumb they are," Terry responded. "We look for them anyway. It's all in the line of duty, right?"

Sharon couldn't believe what she was hearing. What insensitive remarks, she thought. Certainly not in keeping with the idea of serving people in distress. She shook her head. She paused for a few moments outside the door before entering so they wouldn't think she had overheard them. She then sat down at the other desk and began to play back the 911 calls that had come in that evening. Apparently Mark hadn't had any trouble fielding the calls tonight—at least he hadn't said anything to that effect. He hadn't, for instance, asked Sharon to review the calls he'd received. But Mark's shift would be over soon, and she wanted to be familiar with the situation of the lost skier. She put on the earphone, scrolled back to 6 p.m. and pressed the Play button.

* * *

Christ, it's cold, thought Eddie. He took off his glove and tried to zip his jacket up further, but it was already up as high as it would go. *My fingers feel numb. Oh no, if I get frostbite in my hands I might not be able to play the guitar any more! Why didn't I take those matches from the restaurant last night?   Then I could make a fire ... Doesn't anybody care that I'm not there?   Where are all my friends?   I need help!*

He brought his watch close to his face but couldn't make out the time.   His fingers were too numb to press the tiny button for the light.   He reached into his jacket for the plastic case containing his ski pass which was still hanging on a lanyard around his neck.   Using the edge of the case, he was able to depress the little button for the light on the watch bezel.   It was a few minutes after 11 p.m.

My pants got wet when I was looking for my glasses 'cause I was in the snow. How long can someone survive out here, if they're wet? I love snow. The snow used to be my friend. Where are all my friends?

Eddie looked up at the sky. It was dark, clear and cold. The stars were out, his nearsightedness turning them into large, glistening orbs.   There were no other lights, no sounds besides the wind, and his own footsteps slogging through snow and brush. Certainly no sign of another human. It had to be in the low 20's, he thought, but the cold wasn't bothering him quite as much as it had earlier. His brain felt sluggish though. Still, he had moments of lucidity, during which he mulled over his predicament. *I better keep moving, keep trying to find my way out of here. I'll have to come to a road, how could I not? It's a frickin' ski resort, there's got to be a road somewhere around here.   Wonder what all those guys are doing now? Didn't they notice I wasn't there? Of course they noticed. Fred, Mario, they would know I wasn't there. Larry would know. Kathryn would know. Rich and Cheryl, and Marco and Ross, I skied with them, they would've said hey, where's Eddie, at dinner maybe. I called Mario twice. I wonder why he didn't answer his phone?*

He pressed onward, slowly. He was virtually blind without his glasses.

If I keep following the stream I'll get out of here. The stream has to be flowing down, with gravity. I'll just keep following it and I'll come to a road, for sure. I'll come to a road, I'll come to a road, I'll come to a road ...

Though he kept telling himself help was on the way, another part of him didn't believe it. Eddie was never one to rely on others to help him; since he was a kid, he always wanted to do things on his own, be independent. Perhaps it was because he had felt let down so many times by others. It wasn't always their fault, of course. For instance, when he was nine or so, his best friend Jamie Frye moved away, and left Eddie with no one to play with. It wasn't Jamie's fault. His father or mother probably got a job in another state so they had to move ...

How odd that he should think about Jamie now, when he was lost in the woods on a lonely mountain in the middle of the night. He couldn't remember the last time he had thought about Jamie. After his only friend had left, Eddie had been truly alone. Oh, he had his sister Christine, sure. And his parents. But no friends. Not one. In fact, he hadn't really had anyone he thought of as a real friend until he got the job at the Post Office, and met Fred, and joined the Long Island Ski Group. Fred had gotten him back into skiing. They took lessons all the time to improve their skills. Eddie had been on every one of Fred's ski trips. Now, he had many friends. He really felt like he belonged.

Where are they now?

* * *

"Fred, you need to call someone in Eddie's family to tell them what's going on," said Ted.

"Oh, geez. Oh, geez," said Fred. "Who am I gonna call? I guess his mother, right? He lives downstairs from her in the basement apartment. Jesus Christ, what am I gonna say?"

"Do you have her phone number?" asked Ted.

"Uh, I should have it. I should have it. Yeah. It should be on the emergency contact list. Yeah." Fred reached for the plastic cup filled with ice and Scotch. He took a sip and placed the cup back on the table. "Ted. I don't know if I can do it. I can't talk to her. I'm too upset. I'm already a nervous wreck with Mario and all." He took another drink. "Ted, do you think you could call her for me? 'Cause you were already on the phone with the Search and Rescue people, you know more than I do about what they said. You can talk to his mom better than I can."

Ted groaned. "Okay. All right, I'll call her. But can you go find her number for me now, because it's already after one in the morning back home."

* * *

Jesse, Jon, Dan and Jared arrived back at the snow safety office, pulling off knit caps and unzipping jackets. They had located a snowboarder track out in Rick's Basin, as well as a fresh skier track. The next plan was for Jesse to tow out Jared and Andrew as far as the North Boundary Traverse, using ropes tied to a snowmobile. Once there they would check for the tracks Jesse had seen earlier. They left the snow safety office again, arriving at their next search location at 11:23 p.m., when they radioed in to Mandy. (It was essential that Mandy, as dispatcher, know who was where at all times during the search.)

"Do you think they'll find him in time?" Mandy asked Bev, when they were alone in the office. "He's got to be hypothermic by now."

Bev sighed. "Every minute that goes by, his brain is cooling and he's thinking less quickly and efficiently."

"Exactly," replied Mandy. "I can still quote my old textbook: 'When the body temperature drops to between 96 and 94 degrees, fine motor coordination is impaired. Between 95 and 92 degrees, gross motor coordination is affected, and the victim will begin tripping, stumbling and falling.'"

"Yes," said Bev. "The muscles become stiff because the body's beginning to freeze. The thing that really worries me, is that if he made it all the way down the canyon, he's going to be near South Leigh Creek—just like Andrew showed us on the map on his phone."

"I don't know the area very well," said Mandy. "Is that creek fairly straight, or not?"

"It's not straight at all," replied Bev. "It's very winding. And in the winter, you get a lot of snow bridges going over it, and if you're walking around down there you could easily fall through one of those snow bridges and end up in the creek."

"That's even more likely to happen in the dark."

"Yes, of course."

Mandy thought it was about time to check in with Terry Diamond. "Hi Terry, this is Mandy Jones from Targhee Ski Patrol, do you have any updates for us?"

"Hi Mandy, thanks for calling. Uh, the guy has not called back, so... I don't really have any additional information, other than the description I gave you earlier from the ski group leader."

Mandy looked at Bev and shook her head, indicating the lack of news. "Did you try sending a text message to the MP?" she asked.

"No, actually, I didn't." Terry was slightly embarrassed that he hadn't thought of sending a text message. "That's a good idea," he said. "I'll do that now."

"Of course, we don't know if he lost his phone, or maybe the battery is low. But sometimes even if you're low on power, a text can still get through."

"Right," said Terry, typing out the text message.

"If he texts you back," Mandy went on, "maybe you could get his coordinates from pinging the phone."

"We're not, uh, Idaho dispatch doesn't have that capability I don't think," said Diamond. He knew Idaho dispatch had not had that capability the previous year, but it was possible that now they did. No one had informed him if that was so, however.

When Terry was finished composing the text message to Eddie, he read it aloud to Mandy: "This is Commander for SAR. Please call 911 if you get this message."

"That seems fine. I hope he receives it," Mandy said. She knew that she was the low person on the totem pole, but her concern over the possibility of Ed being affected by hypothermia prodded her to continue.

"Terry," she said, "Jon Alexander, our ski patrol assistant director, was asking why your people didn't stage down at the bottom of South Leigh Canyon."

There was a pause on the other end, then Diamond spoke: "Well, in view of our limited resources, and the fact that the skier originated from Targhee, we decided it would be better to stage at Targhee. Have they, uh, have they found any tracks?"

"They have been out to a few different locations," she replied. "Right now they're checking out some tracks that were found earlier to see where they go."

"Okay. Please keep me posted, I'll be here."

"Definitely."

When she hung up, she gave Bev an exasperated look.

"What are they doing on their end?" Bev asked.

"Nothing. All this time they've just been waiting around for the MP to call them back. They finally got around to sending him a text message just now. But really—how ridiculous to think he's going to call back. It's been almost four hours since his last contact."

"What are they thinking over there? Most likely the poor guy can't get a signal," Bev remarked. "Or maybe his phone is dead. Either way, you're right. He's not going to be calling."

"Or," said Mandy, "if he is hypothermic, he might be too confused at this point to even remember how to make a call."

"True," said Bev. "Or if his fingers are frozen, he may not be able to punch the numbers in. But our boys don't seem very concerned about that."

"No they don't. But they should be, in my opinion."

"Mine too," said Bev. "It's in the 20's, it's definitely cold enough out for someone to become hypothermic. And didn't the ski group leader say the MP doesn't have any backcountry gear?"

"Right. So he's basically just out there in his daytime ski clothes. He's got to be freezing by now."

"I would be," said Bev.

"If you and I were in charge, what would we do?" asked Mandy.

"I would have done what Jon Alexander suggested, take some snowmobiles down to South Leigh and search from there. As long as the MP didn't get injured on the way down, then he's way closer to the canyon bottom, at this point, than he is to Targhee."

The radio crackled and Mandy answered it. Andrew reported that a ski track and a snowmobile track met up then diverged: the ski track veered west toward Quakie Ridge and the snowmobile veered to the north, in the direction of South Leigh Canyon.

"Jack and Dan are out at Quakie Ridge," Mandy told him, "I'll let you know what they find. Good work Andrew." She signed off, but a couple of minutes later Andrew radioed back again: "Mandy, now I'm following the skier tracks. They changed direction toward the north. Now it looks like he's using poles, and dragging his skis behind him."

Mandy: "They could tell he was dragging his ski equipment, which is kind of an indication of poor judgement, maybe some disorientation due to cold."

She grimaced. "Okay, thanks Andrew. Keep following them and report back."

Meanwhile, Jack and Dan reported from Quakie Ridge that they had found no visible tracks, nor had there been any response to their call-outs.

A minute later, Andrew reported by radio again: "Mandy? That boot pack we were following turned into a skier track again. It's heading towards the thicker woods going down toward South Leigh Canyon."

"What do you think," asked Mandy. "Do you think that's his track?"

"Probably," said Andrew. "It's fresh. And it's basically following the fall line down the mountain, which would make sense."

"So he's probably down in the canyon by this time," Mandy said.

"Yeah. But we should keep following the track and see where it goes."

"Be safe," Mandy replied. "Remember, Jon said don't go past the ridge. He doesn't want you and Jared going down that chute at night. And neither do I."

"Okay." Andrew signed off.

Over at Rick's Basin, Jon and Jesse conferred while Jesse's German Shepherd Mickey prowled the area. "Well, Dan reported there's nothing up at Quakie," Jon said as he panned his flashlight over the area they had just covered.

"He called out?" asked Jesse.

"Yeah. Nothing. No response."

"Look," said Jesse, "When I was over at the North Boundary, like I told you before, I saw snowboarder tracks and I saw skier tracks. The thing is, the skier tracks went right over the cat track. Like he didn't stop or anything. So he probably didn't see the 'closed' signs." Jesse watched Mickey sniffing around for a moment, then checked his watch. It was coming on to midnight and they had exhausted the possible locations within the resort where the lost skier could be.

"So you're thinking he's definitely down in South Leigh then," Jon said.

"Yeah."

"Okay ... Andrew and Jared are following the track in that direction. But I'm only letting them go as far as the precipice. I don't want anyone skiing down that gully."

"But what about this," Jesse said. "What if we went down to the canyon from further up on the ridge? It would be fairly safe I think. I'd be willing to do it. Will you go with me?"

"No," replied Jon. "Not at night Jesse. I'm not going to allow that."

Jesse nodded. He was Site Commander as far as Teton County Idaho SAR went, but as a Targhee ski patroller he was under Jon's command.

"Okay, whatever you think," he responded. "C'mon Mickey, good boy," he called to the German Shepherd, who was still sniffing the area for clues. "Time to go back to base."

* * *

"Heat, cold (especially wet cold), and altitude can all have physiological effects on the brain, causing interference with safe judgments, or producing irrational behavior. The inexperienced or unprepared may suffer the effects within two or three hours, even at moderate temperatures and elevations." —William G. Syrotuck, Analysis of Lost Person Behavior, page 10.

"Hello, Mrs. McCaul?" Ted stood up when she answered the phone. He had never met Eddie's mother and didn't know what to expect. Would she become hysterical? He hoped not. "Yes, this is Ted Knowlton, I'm a friend of your son Eddie."

"Hello, Ted. Are you with Eddie's ski group?"

"Yes ma'am, I am, and I'm sorry to call so late."

"No, it's fine, I'm just watching television, but is Eddie all right?"

Ted scratched his head and said, "That's why I'm calling. You see, we got word that Eddie became lost while the ski group was at Grand Targhee today."

"Got lost? What do you mean? Eddie never gets lost."

"Yes ma'am," said Ted, "but the visibility at Targhee today was very bad, lots of snow and fog. Most of the group actually quit pretty early in the afternoon. Apparently Eddie kept skiing by himself, and he called 911 about 7:30 tonight to say he was lost."

"He called 911!" Eddie's mother sounded incredulous.

"Yes, and that was the right thing for him to do," said Ted. "Right now Ski Patrol and Search and Rescue are out looking for him. We just wanted to let you know."

"Well, please forgive me Ted," she said, "I'm a little bit confused, or maybe a lot confused. You're telling me that Eddie is lost at a ski resort?"

"Well, he might be somewhere in the ski area, or he might have skied out of bounds by accident and ended up outside of the resort. We don't really know. We're waiting to hear back from the Ski Patrol."

"Oh my goodness—"

"Mrs. McCaul, we don't want to alarm you, it's just that we wanted to let someone in his family know what was going on. I can call you back as soon as he's found ..."

"Oh, please, please call me as soon as you find him! Will you?"

"Yes, definitely. Again, I'm really sorry to have disturbed you so late, and I'll call again as soon as I have more information."

"Thank you Ted, thank you so much. My Eddie is lost, I just can't believe this ..."

"Well, it could've happened to anyone, Mrs. McCaul," Ted replied, trying to think of something to say that would make her feel better. "Listen, I need to keep the line open for Search and Rescue to call me back, so—"

"Yes, yes of course. Please call me as soon as you can, Ted, all right?"

"Yes ma'am. I will, goodbye."

* * *

Clay Striver: "No IC [Incident Commander] was ever formally established."

Don Oscar grabbed the remote from the coffee table and clicked off the TV. Glancing at his watch he saw it was after 11:30. He wondered why he hadn't heard from Clay. Evidently there was nothing to report as yet. He didn't know that Striver had never reported to the site, and had only spoken with Jesse O'Leary and Terry Diamond on the phone.

Oscar decided he'd better notify Tom Catalin, a senior member of the Board of Directors of Teton County Wyoming SAR, that there was a Wyoming search in progress. Catalin answered the phone in a sleepy voice, apparently he had already gone to bed.

"Who's on site?" asked Catalin after Oscar had briefed him.

"Idaho SAR and Grand Targhee Ski Patrol, and Striver."

"What's the status of the search?"

Oscar hesitated. "I'm waiting to hear back from Clay," he said, "so I'm not sure yet."

"Who else do we have from the team, besides Clay?"

"No one."

"What?" Catalin sounded surprised. "Didn't you page out the team?"

Oscar knew he didn't handle criticism very well, and he tried to keep the ire out of his voice. "We didn't feel it was necessary. Idaho has their team, ski patrol is there, Jesse O'Leary—they're capable people," he replied, more gruffly than he had intended.

"Don, you know perfectly well this is Wyoming's responsibility. The missing person originated from Targhee. Our team should have been sent out immediately."

Don tapped his fingers on the side of the TV remote. Catalin obviously didn't understand the situation.

"Relax Tom, it's being handled. And we already have the heli on standby. If the guy doesn't get found, or walk out, we'll just go get him in the morning with the heli. It'll be a lot easier."

"Well, that wouldn't be my choice," Catalin said. "Can you keep me posted on this?"

"Sure," Oscar replied, relieved that the conversation appeared to be over. "I'll get back to you when I have more information." He said goodbye and went to the kitchen to pour himself a soda. It was quiet in the house —too quiet. His wife had taken their son with her to her mother's house for a few days. She was doing that a lot lately. It was probably only a matter of time before she would want to call it quits on their marriage. Hey, there was nothing he could do. Once a woman decides something, that's it. He would just have to deal with it. As long as he could still see his son, he could handle it.

Oscar ran over in his mind what he'd need to do tomorrow, which was Wednesday: first thing, if this skier didn't turn up tonight, he'd be meeting Clay and Len at the hangar so they could take off at first light. And he had to remember to sign his son up for that indoor rock climbing class.

When the phone rang, he knew who it would be. "What's up Clay?"

"Not much Don. Listen, the MP hasn't been found. No surprise there, right? So why don't you and me and Len meet at the hangar at 7:30 a.m.?"

"Yeah, good. We'll just go up in the heli and grab him . . . thanks Clay, see you in the morning."

Don Oscar: "I think the person in charge of Search and Rescue Wyoming was Clay Striver ... I'm not really sure it was our incident to begin with. I believe ... while they were all searching, they were in Rick's Basin, which is part of Targhee, and the Ski Patrol was working in their area that they control, so Clay Striver was assisting with that situation."

* * *

Andrew and Jared paused at the edge of the precipice that led down a steep chute into South Leigh Canyon. "Jon said not to go any farther than this," said Jared.

"I know," Andrew replied. Even though he would have skied down the chute at night if Jon had asked him to, he knew why Jon had prohibited it. This was avalanche territory and it was risky, so he felt secretly relieved to have an excuse not to continue.

"I think we should go down," said Jared. "Let's radio Jon. If the two of us go down together it would be safer. The tracks are going that way, look." He lifted his ski pole and pointed down the chute, where the lost skier's post-holing, and the dragging of his skis, was evident. "He's been walking. He couldn't have gotten far on foot," Jared continued. "I think we're close; we could probably catch up to him."

"We can't," said Andrew, "Jon said to come back in so let's go. You have your skins?"

The boys were now downslope and needed to hike up the mountain to where Jon could pick them up with the snowmobile. In order to ascend slopes on downhill skis, one must attach "skins" to the skis which will provide enough traction to go uphill.

They took their packs off and removed the skins. The skins were very loosely folded, with plastic linings over them to preserve the adhesive backing. They ripped off the linings and tossed them on the snow. Most skiers would remove their skis to attach skins, but the boys took a shortcut. Each of them shook the excess snow off, hoisted one leg, and stuck the ski tail in the snow so it was vertical. They fitted the wire loop over the tips of their skis while still holding the end clamp. By reversing the move and sticking the tip in the snow with the leg behind, they could hook the clamp ends over the ski tails, all accomplished without removing the skis. With skins attached, now they could easily go uphill. Jon would pick them up when they reached the snowmobile-accessible terrain at the North Boundary Traverse.

"You know what doesn't make sense to me? Why didn't Idaho send people to the bottom of the canyon first, and work their way up?" said Andrew while adjusting the tail clamp on his left ski.

"Maybe they did," Jared said.

"You'd think someone would have mentioned it, though, if they did," Andrew said. "But the MP has obviously gone down in that direction... he could be at the bottom by now. They could still go with snowmobiles up the summer road."

"Yeah," Jared replied. "That would be a good idea. But don't you think they already thought of that? They're professionals, man."

"Maybe they did it and didn't tell us. We're on a need-to-know basis," said Andrew, and they both laughed.

"You ready?" asked Jared.

Andrew took one last glance down the chute. "Yeah."

They adjusted their packs and began skinning back up the mountain.

* * *

Terry dialed Clay Striver's cell phone. If Striver thought it was a good idea, Idaho SAR had the two snowmobiles—Jack and Dan could go back down to the canyon and take them up the summer road and determine whether the skier was within earshot. It was certainly worth a try at this point. Anything was worth a try ...

Clay Striver: "As I recall he said, well, if you think it's appropriate or safe do you want a couple of us, because they only have two machines ... and I because of the level of urgency, because of the limited probability of success, because of searcher safety—I said no, I don't think it's appropriate."

* * *

"When lost or overdue, skiers either keep moving to stay warm, build snow shelters, or break into structures. [Barry] Mitchell found 30-45% moved at night."
> —Lost Person Behavior by Robert J. Koester, page 231

Eddie was intent on staying calm. He had already had a number of anxiety attacks and he realized he had to control his mind. He focused on his breathing, and his slow steps through the woods. Without his glasses his ears had to be his eyes, and every sound jumped out with an intensity he'd never experienced before. The swishing of his boots through the snow, the crack of a stepped-on twig or branch, the distant call of what was probably a coyote. He wondered if coyotes ate humans. He knew they ate cats—a cousin of his from Connecticut had said that had happened to her cat. But he wasn't at all sure if coyotes would attack a man. *Maybe if there was a pack of them. Maybe if they were hungry enough.*

All of a sudden he heard an unfamiliar sound. He stopped. There it was again! It was low kind of rumbling growl. *Shit! Is there a fucking bear? Shit!* He heard the sound again, and it did seem closer. A coyote was one thing—a frigging bear was something else. *Jesus Christ! I'm going to get eaten by a bear! Jesus Christ!* He hit himself on the chest with his gloved hand. *Stop it! Stop it Eddie! Don't panic! Stay calm!*

He saw the vague outline of what he hoped was a stout branch lying to his left. He reached down to pick it up. The branch had about a 2 inch diameter. Yes, he could use this. He broke off some smaller twigs from its base and grasped it with his left hand. In his right hand he let one ski pole drop to the ground but kept the other, making sure its strap was secured around his wrist.

If a bear attacked, he resolved to defend himself to the best of his ability. He would not run—that might attract the bear, who would think it was an animal. Also, if he started thrashing through the woods, he might trip and hurt himself. His heart pounded. His fear seemed to bring back some ability to think rationally, which had been dissipating somewhat as his body temperature cooled.

If a bear comes, I'll just stick my ski pole in its eye. Or its throat. That's what I'll do! But, I can't see. What if I miss and I just make it mad! What if it kills me?

Eddie's emotional state wavered between confidence and despair. As despair won out, he fought the urge to cry. *If something happens to me, who's going to bring the groceries to Mrs. McGill? I bring her groceries every Thursday. She's a nice old lady. It's hard for her to go shopping, she can hardly walk. Mom, I'm sorry, I really screwed up ... Dad ... Christine ... if something happens to me ... Mom who's going to take care of you? Who's going to bring you to the hospital for your treatments?* His tears flowed more quickly now, and became frozen rivulets that stuck to his face in the cold night air.

* * *

Dan and Jack arrived back at the snow safety office just before midnight. Mandy recorded their return in the log. Within five minutes Jesse walked in with his dog Mickey at his heels. Jesse had just toweled down the animal, and was still praising him for a good night's work.

Clay Striver: "It was vague in my understanding of exactly what the ... Idaho SAR personnel were doing during the Rick's Basin search effort. At one time I was under the impression that they were actually down at the Driggs Emergency Services Building and there was some discussion of snowmobile searching. I wasn't sure whether that meant they were up South Leigh or whether that meant they were up in Rick's Basin."

The desk phone rang; it was Terry Diamond.

"Hi Terry," Mandy said, "Jesse is back, do you want to talk to him?" Receiving an affirmative reply, she handed the phone to Jesse.

"Hey Terry... yeah, the tracks are definitely leading down into South Leigh... are you... what?"

Mandy and Bev watched Jesse's face as he spoke with the Idaho SAR commander. He looked puzzled. "They're going to suspend the search?" he asked. Mandy gasped.

"Oh no!" said Bev softly.

Not one prone to demonstrative behavior, Jesse's surprise was apparent. He listened to Terry's explanation, then said "I need to talk to Clay. Let me give him a ring ... a conference call with Don? Okay. Good idea. I'll stand by." He hung up and shook his head. He cleared his throat and addressed everyone assembled in the office—Mandy, Bev, Dan and Jack. "Wyoming is going to suspend the ground search and go get him with the heli in the morning."

"What! Really?" said Mandy and Bev simultaneously.

"You're kidding!" said Jack.

"I know," said Jesse, "it doesn't make sense." He took his cellphone out of his pocket and dialed Clay's number, walking out into the hallway as he heard Clay's voice on the other end.

"Clay," said Jesse, "We're pretty sure the MP is down in the canyon. We can take the Idaho snowmobiles up the road at the bottom of South Leigh, we could be there in ninety minutes. We can just go as far as the trailhead, or we could tow a couple people on skins part way and search a little ways up."

"Jesse," replied Clay, "I already told you. It's useless to search at night. The helicopter is the best tool for this search. Tell the patrol to stand down. Don and I will be going up in the ship at first light, we'll grab the MP and be out of there."

Jesse tugged on his beard. He knew there was nothing more he could do—technically this was a Wyoming search, and as a representative of Wyoming SAR Striver had authority over how to proceed. Jesse signed off and walked back into the office. His cellphone rang. It was Terry Diamond, advising Jesse that Don Oscar was on the line as well, ready to proceed with the conference call.

"Jesse, why are you so sure that the tracks your team saw belong to the missing person," Oscar asked.

"It appears to be a lost skier because he's walking. There are post-holing tracks and it appears he was dragging his skis behind him. The tracks continue down the gully but Jon didn't want our people going down there at night. So we had to come back."

"Okay. Look, we appreciate the efforts you guys made. But I think the smartest move is to go get the guy in the morning. I've already got Len Jameson on standby with the heli. Clay and I will go up with him at first light. We'll get this done in less than an hour."

"If you think that's best, Don," said Diamond.

"Don," said Jesse, "we could shoot up the summer road in South Leigh with a couple of snowmobiles and just see—."

"Look, Jesse. This guy is an adult," Oscar said. "He's not a kid. He's not a pregnant woman or some vulnerable person. He was a jerk and ducked a rope. He took a risk. He shouldn't have done that and he'll have to bide his time out there till we arrive."

Jesse walked back into the First Aid Room, holding the cellphone to his ear. "Right," he said, as Mandy, Bev, Dan and Jack looked on. "We'll go get him in the morning." He signed off and looked at the wondering faces of the others in the room.

"What's up Jesse?" asked Dan. Mandy and Bev exchanged glances; it sounded as if Jesse had not been able to convince Wyoming to continue with the search.

"That's it. Wyoming says to stand down," Jesse said.

Jack spoke up: "But really, why? There's still more we can do! We could approach the canyon from the bottom, he's probably there by now."

"Look," Jesse said, "I don't make the rules. I asked, but Clay denied permission to continue the search from the bottom with snowmobiles. Don Oscar says stand down. So we stand down. He said if it was a pregnant lady or a twelve year old kid we could go after them, but it's not. If the guy has to spend the night in the cold and lose a few toes, that's how it has to be."

Mandy and Bev exchanged pained glances.

"Wow," said Jack. Dan looked down at the floor.

Voices sounded in the hallway. A few moments later Jon came in with Andrew and Jared, whom he had towed back in to base from the North Boundary Traverse. The boys' cheeks were still flushed with the effort of skinning back up the mountain, and snow clung to their pants and boots.

"Well now we know where he is!" said Jon in an upbeat voice. "Time to go to Plan B." His statement was greeted with dead silence from Mandy, Bev, Jack, Dan and Jesse. He looked at them questioningly.

"Jon," Jesse said, "I just got off the phone with Don Oscar and Terry Diamond. Oscar says we have to stand down. They've decided they're going to let him hang out down there for the night, and go get him in the heli tomorrow morning."

"What?" Jon said, incredulous. "Why? Obviously he's down in South Leigh. We take the sleds, park at the trailhead, we can probably find him and bring him in tonight. Did they really say to stand down?"

"Yeah. I mean, if it was a twelve year old kid, or a pregnant lady... but Oscar said 'he's a grown man.' So if the guy has to spend the night in the cold and lose a few toes, that's how it has to be."

"Unbelievable!" said Jon. "Well, okay. We've thoroughly covered the resort area, so it's Wyoming's call at this point. We're done."

"Wow," said Jack again.

Jon sighed deeply. "You're all excused. Thanks a lot for your help. We did all we can do. Good job, everyone."

Sitting at the desk with pen still in hand, Mandy's brow was furrowed as she thought about the lost skier suffering the effects of hypothermia. And surely he would be frightened over being stranded in the wilderness all night. She couldn't believe they were calling off the search. Jesse seemed to agree so readily to suspend the search, and Jon too. Were they afraid to argue with Wyoming? Afraid to insist on continuing the search? Jon had been right, it should be time to move on to Plan B: Drive back down Ski Hill Rd to Driggs, head north to Tetonia, go up the dirt road at Hatches Corners, and take off from the trailhead where hikers park their vehicles. Jack Stills interrupted her thoughts.

"This is just nuts. We ought to bring an ambulance to the trailhead. We can safely continue. At least we could locate some more tracks—"

Mandy: "They had vast knowledge of that terrain and felt comfortable going there."

Jon put his hand on Jack's shoulder. "I appreciate your willingness to continue Jack, but the fact is, this is not our call. It's Wyoming's call. We have to accept it. I just want to mention to everyone, we don't freelance. We are now officially done for the night."

The mood in the snow safety office was somber as everyone assembled their gear and made ready to depart. Jon phoned the front desk and arranged for rooms overnight at Targhee for himself and Jesse. They might be needed in the morning to assist in the rescue.

Dan, Bev and Jack began putting their jackets on, and went out to load the snowmobiles back onto the trailer for the return trip to Driggs. Dan radioed Terry Diamond and told him they were heading back. After he signed off, Bev turned to the men and said "We need to go down to South Leigh and search from there."

"Yeah," agreed Jack from the back seat. "You up for it, Dan?"

Dan shook his head. "Look, this is not our search anymore. Actually, it never was Idaho's search. Technically we were just there to assist Wyoming and Targhee Ski Patrol."

"Yes," interrupted Bev, "But this just doesn't make sense, Dan. The poor man is freezing out there! He might die! He's from New York and he doesn't know the area—"

"We could easily drive the snowmobiles up as far as the trailhead," said Jack. "Why don't we?"

Dan was adamant. "It's not a good idea, you guys. Remember, Jon said 'don't freelance.' And these aren't even our personal snowmobiles, they belong to Idaho SAR. So..."

Dan Van Horst: *"We were driving back down towards Driggs and talking with the Stills, and they mentioned that we should go up and search South Leigh Canyon. And I responded to them that we were operating under authority from the Jackson Search and Rescue team,* *and they did not give us that authority to go up and were suspending the search for the evening. So we did not have jurisdictional ability to go up and search on our own. If we were, we were going as private citizens and not as our Search and Rescue team."*

Jon Alexander was alone in the snow safety office; everyone else had left. But he had one more task remaining before he could leave: he needed to fill out the Relative Urgency Guidelines form. He went to the file cabinet and got out a copy of the form, and sat down at the desk recently vacated by Mandy to assess the numerical score that would indicate the degree of urgency of the search. The guidelines had been prepared and disseminated by NASAR, the National Association for Search and Rescue. The paragraph at the top of the form states: "On the following chart, the lower the numerical rating, the higher the relative urgency becomes. A total score of 7 would indicate the highest urgency and a total score of 21 would indicate the lowest urgency. The chart is intended only as a guide. The Incident Commander in the process of establishing urgency must also evaluate all other factors bearing on the incident."

Jon circled the numbers corresponding to what was known about the MP and this incident, in the categories of age, medical condition, number of subjects, subject experience profile, equipment profile, terrain/hazards profile. He came up with a score of 7 to 9, indicating this incident was of the highest urgency. But Wyoming had said to stand down.

Jon had done all he was authorized to do. He threw the pen down and pushed his chair away from the desk. He grabbed his jacket, flipped off the lights and left the room, slamming the door behind him.

* * *

Recorded Phone Conversation Between Jackson Dispatcher And Sheriff Jennings, 12:29 A.M., January 20

Sheriff Jennings: Hello?

Dispatcher: You did say you wanted [to be] called right? This is Karen at Dispatch. They did not find him. They found tracks going into the south area of Leigh Canyon just north of the ski area.

J: Okay.

D: So they are not going to try and go in and find him tonight. They are going to fly at first light and look again.

J: Now, I'd heard that they were going to try and talk him out if they got ahold of somebody that knew the area. Is that not available to them?

D: Apparently not, they lost contact with him around 7 o'clock tonight.

J: Well, okay.

D: That's all I know.

J: Yeah, okay.

D: They'll fly it in the morning.

J: Well, if the guy is dressed to ski he's probably dressed to survive the night, so ...

D: Let's hope so.

J: Okay Karen, well thank you.

D: All right bye.

J: All right, bye bye.

END OF CONVERSATION

* * *

Deputy Dammer drove to the Parkway Inn for the second time that night. She had been hoping to be able to deliver some good news. No such luck. As she pulled up to the parking lot, she could see Fred, Larry and Kathryn sitting in the chairs by the window in the lobby. A partly emptied bottle of Scotch was the table centerpiece. With the soft lighting, tasteful antiques and comfortable armchairs, the interior of the Parkway looked inviting from outside, the very picture of a cozy winter retreat. But Edward was spending the night alone in the Wyoming wilderness on a cold, dark January night. Hopefully he had had the sense to build himself a snow cave. From what Fred had said earlier, however, it seemed Edward was not an experienced backcountry skier or camper. He had no equipment with him, no food, no emergency provisions of any kind. It was doubtful he would think of building a snow cave.

Deputy Dammer hoped Edward could keep his wits about him and not fall into the creek that ran along the bottom of South Leigh Canyon. It was a very winding creek that followed the base of the mountain for some length—wide at times, and elsewhere narrowing to the size of a stream, perhaps eight or nine feet across. It would be very dark in the woods, and difficult to see the water because of the snow bridges. She hoped that Edward might be able to at least hear the stream, even if he couldn't see it. Because if he fell in, or even got just part of himself wet by slipping into it, the chances of him suffering hypothermia would be greatly increased. She prayed that wouldn't happen. But that bad feeling in her gut hadn't gone away.

Fred jumped up and ran outside when he saw Dammer's cruiser pull up. He peered into the passenger window. The seat was, of course, empty.

"I don't have him," said Dammer, rolling down the window. "I'm sorry. Let's go inside and talk."

Fred followed her back into the Parkway's lobby. Both Larry and Kathryn were standing now. "I'm sorry, he hasn't been found yet," said Dammer. "But I'd like to talk to you all a little more. Can we please sit down?"

Larry grabbed a straight-backed chair from another table and pulled it closer so that Dammer could join them. "Isn't there any news at all, Deputy?" asked Kathryn.

"Not yet I'm afraid, but we're still hopeful." Dammer said.

"Care for a drink," asked Fred, refilling his glass.

"No thank you," Dammer replied. "I'm on duty."

"Oh, right, sorry," said Fred.

"Where is Ted," asked Dammer.

"He's upstairs. He's waiting for any calls from Search and Rescue."

Kathryn sat forward in her seat and looked intently at the deputy. "Have they found anything useful? Like, did they find his tracks?"

Dammer wondered how much information she should give out. She stalled. "Well, basically," she said, "they did find some tracks going out of bounds. But there's no way to be absolutely certain that those are Eddie's tracks."

"Well who else's would they be," asked Larry. "Did anyone else call 911 and say they were lost? Are there any other lost skiers out there? The tracks have got to be his!"

"It's not quite that simple," the deputy replied. "Yes, there was fresh snowfall and the tracks were fresh, but you have to realize that sometimes people ski out of bounds on purpose. The locals do it all the time. So the tracks might belong to Eddie, but they also might belong to a local who, for instance, might have skied out of bounds on purpose because they knew where they were, and they knew how to get to where they were going."

Larry shook his head, remarking "I don't know, it seems like if ski tracks were found going out of bounds, and Eddie has been calling into 911, those are probably his tracks. So then, can't they just follow the tracks and find him?"

"The Ski Patrol followed the tracks as far as they could," replied Dammer, "to the edge of a precipice. They weren't able to continue down the mountain because of avalanche danger. Obviously, it's also dark out, so visibility is reduced."

"Are there a lot of avalanches here?" asked Kathryn.

"There are more than there used to be," said Dammer. "Avalanche danger is a pretty common hazard in these parts. Basically, the patrol has to check every day on what the avalanche forecast is. They actually will close parts of the mountain at certain times. Other times they'll fire explosives to trigger the avalanche on purpose, so they can control the circumstances. I don't know if you're aware of this, but during an avalanche the snow becomes much harder, like cement. So it's a bigger danger than you might imagine."

"No, I didn't realize that," said Kathryn.

Dammer leaned forward and took out her notebook and pen. "Tell me more about Edward," she said. "What kind of person is he?"

"Eddie is a very close friend of mine," said Fred, his speech somewhat slurred as a result of the alcohol he'd been consuming. "I've known Eddie for, like, what, fifteen years?"

"You met him at the post office, right?" asked Kathryn.

"Have you been skiing with him that whole time?" asked the deputy.

"Yeah, pretty much," said Fred. "I got him back into skiing. When he started up again, he was like a beginner, you know. He would get on skis, he could go down the mountain, make some turns, you know. His level was like, low to intermediate. But then when he got with us, and started skiing with us good skiers, he got better real fast."

Larry jumped in, "One time when I was taking ski lessons I fell, and right then Cola zipped past me, and when he was flying by he yelled out that I should get a better helmet. He looks like a damn good skier! I'll never be that good." He laughed.

"I've never seen a trail he couldn't handle," said Kathryn.

"That's Cola, all right." Fred took another sip of his drink.

Larry found himself staring at Fred's glass. It was almost hypnotizing, the way the half-empty glass was backlit from the lamp on the table. The ice was almost melted, small slivers floating in the amber liquid. Larry forced himself out of his trance. "Eddie was very resourceful. A very resourceful individual."

"Resourceful," asked Dammer, "How do you mean?"

"Well, there was this time in Europe," said Larry, crossing and uncrossing his legs, "this is just an example, to demonstrate how competent he is. So, we were in Barcelona, when we went out to the Andorra trip with the ski group, we spent a couple of days in Barcelona. And we were out with a bunch of people and they were shopping, the women were shopping and Eddie said, 'I don't want to do this, I'm going back to the hotel.' I said, 'We'll take a ride back together in the car service.' He said, 'No. I'll take the metro.' He didn't speak Spanish or read Spanish or anything. But he wasn't afraid. He took the metro and made it back before I did. He was a very resourceful individual."

The deputy was writing in her notebook. "He was resourceful," she said, "but he didn't carry a backpack of any kind, with supplies or anything?"

"Why should he," said Fred. "We were skiing at a resort. Nobody has a backpack! Well," he corrected himself, "maybe some of them do, but we don't do that. Why should we? We're skiing at a resort!" he finished, placing his glass on the table with finality.

"Yeah," said Kathryn, "I never saw Eddie skiing with a backpack or even wearing a fanny pack. He just wore that red Coolar jacket.

Everything else was always black. Black pants, black gloves. Black hat. Oh, I think he had yellow goggles."

"Backcountry skiers carry shovels with them that they can use to build snow caves, but Eddie won't be able to do that," Dammer remarked, almost to herself. "A Coolar jacket. Gloves. It sounds like he was dressed for the weather, at least."

"You asked what kind of person he is," said Kathryn. "Well, I would describe Eddie as a very caring person. If someone is in trouble and he can help, he does it. Fred—" she continued, "do you remember the time Eddie rescued Marisa, in Italy?"

"Oh yeah," said Fred, chuckling.

"What happened?" asked Dammer.

"Well," said Fred, "one of the girls got lost and Eddie found her. She was pretty upset. She thought she was lost. She was still in the resort but she was, like, stuck in this loop. It was on the border of Italy and Switzerland."

"She said she didn't even know which country she was in," remarked Kathryn.

"Yeah. And Eddie saw her going around in circles and followed her, so when she stopped she saw him. She told me she'd never forget how he saved her."

"I see," said Dammer. "Well, do you think it's possible Eddie might have dialed 911 just because he was tired and wanted to be towed out on a snowmobile, for instance?"

"Definitely not," said Kathryn emphatically. "You have to realize, if Eddie called 911, he really is in trouble. He would never just call 911 frivolously, do you know what I mean?"

Dammer nodded, jotting this down in her notebook. "Ted mentioned that Eddie might be autistic. Does he have problems communicating?"

"Autistic? I don't know," Kathryn replied. "It's just that he doesn't like to bother anybody unless he has to. And he doesn't like to call attention to himself. If he dialed 911," continued Kathryn, "it was only as a last resort. Eddie is very shy."

"That's right," said Larry. "Cola is the kind of guy who stands around listening to the conversation, but he doesn't participate very much. He isn't a big talker."

"But you said he doesn't have difficulty communicating?" asked Dammer.

"No, oh no, not Eddie," interjected Fred. "He communicates fine. He's the Assistant Shop Steward at the Post Office. He has to go to the union meetings and then come back and tell everybody what they said. He can talk fine, when he wants to."

"Or when he has to," added Kathryn.

* * *

Mark Silver's shift had ended and he had gone home for the night. Sharon Courier was now on duty in the dispatch room of the Teton County Idaho Sheriff's Office, and she was worried. They still hadn't found that lost skier, and it was damned cold out, in her opinion. Maybe not the coldest it had ever been, but still cold enough to cause serious injury to an unprotected person. Low twenties, it felt like. She was pretty sure a New Yorker would consider it quite cold, and probably very scary out in the wilderness. She lived here, and she knew that she herself would be out of her mind with fright if she were in his situation.

She was listening to the 911 calls—just the ones between the skier and Mark Silver—over and over again. At one point she thought the skier had said he was near a stream, but she wasn't sure. She would have to listen to it some more. She knew the danger if he *was* near a stream. If he happened to fall in, the potential for a fatality would be compounded. She wondered why he hadn't been found yet; SAR had surely listened to the recording and heard that part about the stream, and she knew there weren't many streams in the area. But maybe he had wandered away from it? Oh well, there wasn't anything to do but wait.

At 12:30 a.m. Terry Diamond walked into the dispatch room with a woman Sharon did not recognize.

Sharon: "She was taller than me, medium to large build, longer than shoulder length hair, and dark clothes." Sharon had no idea who the woman might be, but the three of them were there when the call came in from Wyoming: the search had been suspended for the night.

"Okay Don," Terry had said on the phone. "Whatever you think is best."

Sharon sighed. They were apparently going to launch an air rescue the following morning, with the helicopter. Wyoming was very big on the use of helicopters. They'd been lobbying to get their own helicopter hangar for years, and now they finally were building one. The new facility would also contain space for Search and Rescue training sessions.

Sharon had never flown in a helicopter. She thought they were rather dangerous and had no desire to do so.

"Sharon, thanks," said Terry. He sounded tired. "I'm going home. See you later."

"Okay Terry, have a good night," said Sharon. Terry and the unidentified woman left the dispatch room. Once they were gone, Sharon held the headset closer to her ear and pressed the "play" button again. She felt sure she was hearing everything. Mark had said, "Okay... can you describe what kind, what area you're in right now?"

Eddie had replied, "Yeah, there's a meadow, there's a meadow here, there's a bunch of, uh, bunch of fallen trees it seems, there's a stream."

Stream. Yes, he definitely said "stream," thought Sharon. She made a notation in the log book.

* * *

Eddie could not feel his fingers. His hands felt like lumps. He looked down and was surprised that he was still wearing his gloves. Suddenly his boot caught in a snowdrift and he fell sideways, landing sidesaddle in the snow. He stayed like that for awhile. It felt good to sit down. He felt a snotsicle forming on his face and decided to blow his nose. He pulled his right glove off by wedging it between his left elbow and his torso. He put his hand in his jacket pocket to feel for the napkin he had saved from breakfast. But he couldn't feel anything with his fingers. Maybe the napkin wasn't there. Or maybe it was in the other pocket. He couldn't pull his jacket around to feel in the other pocket. It was so much effort ... he had to put the glove back on now. He tried to guide his fingers into the correct spaces ... *No, can't do it. They won't go in. It's okay, it feels warmer now. Yes, it's warmer, I don't need the glove. I'll just put it in my pocket. There. It's in my pocket. The glove is in my pocket... wow, look at the snow, how pretty it is! The snow is blue. But snow is supposed to be white. It looks blue now. Blue snow ... hello snow. I love snow ... Oh! I have to get up now. I can't stay like this, my pants will get even more wet! I have to get up.*

With great effort Eddie rallied to his feet and began moving slowly through the woods once again. Suddenly he was falling. His body had crashed through a snow bridge, and he heard the sound of water sloshing. As he slipped further into the frigid current, he felt a sharp pain in his chest. He gasped.

He hadn't thought he was that close to the stream—what had happened? He thrashed around, dropping the big stick he had been using to protect himself from the bear. He still had the ski pole wrapped around his other wrist. He took another step, and the bottom of the pole skidded away from him as it slid on the rocks. The pole's strap came off his wrist as Eddie landed on his knees, on a big rock, while the current gushed on either side of him. He tried to right himself but had lost his sense of equilibrium. In the next moment, he found himself lying on his side as the icy water sloshed over his body. A second sharp pain wracked his sternum, but this one was different—he must have hit a rock. Again he could barely catch his breath. The water was freezing!

With difficulty he got back on his feet, but upon standing, he couldn't orient himself. He couldn't see, nor feel, from which direction he had come. He wanted desperately to get back on land. But which way was it?

* * *

"If you or your organization begins to provide services or treatment, you have a legal duty to continue." —Fundamentals of Search and Rescue, *page 36*

"Let's go down to the trailhead," said Jared. Mandy and Andrew readily agreed. They got into Jared's vehicle and began the 40-minute ride down to South Leigh Canyon. At first they were quiet, listening to the swishing and crunching of the tires on the snow and ice that had accumulated on the road, but soon Jared broke the silence. "Who was the IC on this anyway?"

It was a good question. "IC" stands for Incident Commander. According to the National Association for Search and Rescue, *"Usually, the person in charge of the first arriving units at the scene of an incident assumes the IC role. That person will remain in charge until formally relieved or until transfer of command is accomplished. As incidents grow in size or become more complex, a more highly qualified IC may be assigned by the responsible jurisdiction or agency. Even if other functions are not filled, an IC will always be designated."*

Don Oscar: " ... from my belief I think the people that are first on scene are IC, and until we can get transfer that's how it should work from the IC standpoint."

"That's a good point," said Mandy. "I believe it should have been Terry Diamond. But nobody ever actually said that. No one said, to me anyway, 'Terry Diamond is IC.'"

"Well if he was IC," remarked Andrew, "why was it the Wyoming guy who called off the search?"

"Maybe the Wyoming guy was the actual IC," said Jared.

"He couldn't have been IC. He wasn't even there," Andrew said.

"Well, neither was Terry Diamond," Jared countered.

"Yeah, but at least Terry was at the Idaho Sheriff's Office. Not like the Wyoming guy, Don Oscar. He was, like, in his house."

Jared snorted. "I know, it's crazy, right?"

Mandy said, "There's *so* many things wrong with this. I mean, Wyoming never even showed up, even though it was in their jurisdiction. Then Idaho—I don't know why they never sent anyone down to South Leigh to search from that direction. Why did they stage at Targhee? We really didn't need them, we already had Jon, and Jesse, and you guys, and me sitting dispatch. We didn't need the Idaho people to help search Rick's or Quakie Ridge. The woman, Bev, mostly all she did was sit next to me in dispatch the whole time."

"Yeah, why didn't they go and search from down below while we were searching up top?" asked Andrew. "That would've made much more sense."

Jared said, "Maybe they did send their team down here. We don't know for sure."

"I talked to Terry Diamond a few times during the night, and he never said a word about sending his team down to South Leigh," said Mandy. "I feel so terrible! Edward is probably injured, or severely hypothermic right now." She rubbed her nose with her glove. "It's wrong to abandon the person, especially when you know where they are. Why didn't Jesse argue more with Wyoming about calling it off?"

"You know why. Because Wyoming SAR calls the shots," said Andrew.

"There'll probably be a debriefing later this week about the search," said Jared. "But we can't complain about what happened, because we're not senior patrollers like Jesse."

"Well," said Mandy, "I don't care if nobody wants to listen to me. I'm going to say something anyway."

When they reached the dirt road at Hatches Corners, they made the turn that would lead them to the small clearing where hikers and snowmobilers park their vehicles at the base of South Leigh Canyon. They got out of the car, zipped up their jackets and donned their headlamps. The night was clear and cold. The three of them stood there a moment, listening to the slowly-moving stream, sniffing the icy air. There was just a sliver of moon, and the stars shone brightly above the deserted Western wilderness.

Jared cupped his gloved hands around his mouth and called out, "Edward!" He stretched out the vowels the way his mother used to when she'd call him to come in for dinner when he was a kid. He shouted again, and they listened to the canyon's echo. They walked a little farther up the trail, their boots crunching on the rutted, icy, snow-covered road. They stopped, and Andrew took a turn calling Eddie's name. Mandy got out her whistle and gave two long blasts. Nothing.

"My voice is higher, maybe he'll hear me," said Mandy, and she tried two or three times, waiting about twenty seconds in between shouts. The only response was from the mountains, just another echo cushioned by a ponderous silence.

"Without snowmobiles, there's not much more we can do," Andrew said. "And anyway, I don't think it's a good idea for us to go up the mountain at night."

"My friend does it all the time," said Jared. "I've done it once or twice with him."

"Well, yeah, I've gone with my friends too. But not by myself," said Andrew, a bit defensively.

"I wish we could do it, but we shouldn't," interjected Mandy. "Even if we had the snowmobiles, Jon said not to freelance."

"Really, why didn't those Idaho guys go up there," Andrew asked. "They usually like doing hot-shot stuff like that. They grab any chance to ride a snowmobile up the mountain." He looked at his watch. "It's quarter after one. Let's try one more time," he suggested. He motioned to Jared, whose voice seemed to carry the best. Jared lifted his gloved hands once more and gave a long, drawn out bellow for Edward. They waited. Mandy blew her whistle again. Their efforts were swallowed by the wilderness. They stood there for another minute, then trudged back down the trail toward the car, slowly, as if by lingering they could give the lost skier one more chance.

"Andrew," said Mandy, "what's the temperature?" She pointed to the Grand Teton National Park keychain with a thermometer on it, hanging from the zipper on his jacket.

Andrew pulled the zipper down and brought the thermometer into the beam of his headlamp. "Looks like 15 degrees Fahrenheit," he replied.

"Shit," said Jared. "Pretty cold."

Mandy called out "Edward!" one last time before the three young patrollers piled back into Jared's vehicle for the ride home.

500 yards away, on the other side of the creek, Eddie Cola was lying in the snow. He had been lying down to rest for a few minutes. He was so tired. As he went in and out of consciousness he dreamed vividly of himself as a little boy, and Rags, his Miniature Schnauzer. He was outside in the yard, tossing a stick for Rags to chase. There was a voice calling his name. The voice was his mother, calling him to come in for dinner ...

Chapter 5
The Next Day

Testimony of expert witness Dr. Alan M. Steinman: "The human body requires a relatively tight control of its core body temperature in order to maintain the myriad physiological processes essential for life. When more heat is lost from the body than it can produce through metabolism and retain through clothing, behavior or environmental control, then hypothermia will inevitably occur. Systemic hypothermia will ultimately lead to death if not reversed. The human body attempts to maintain a normal body core temperature in the range of 98.6 degrees F (oral) plus or minus 1 degree F, or 99.6 degrees F (rectal) plus/minus 1 degree F. Hypothermia is medically defined when the core temperature drops below 95 degrees F.

The signs and symptoms of hypothermia vary with body temperature. As core temperature begins to decline from normal levels, the body tries to defend itself by increasing its metabolism to produce more heat, and by decreasing blood flow through the skin, particularly in the extremities, to reduce heat loss to the environment. The body responds to this heat loss by initially increasing metabolic rate to produce more heat. In addition, involuntary shivering occurs to produce significantly more heat. The shivering response becomes maximal around a core temperature of 90-91 degrees F. However, as the core temperature continues to fall, metabolic rate declines, since the biochemical processes necessary to maintain cellular energy production become progressively less responsive. Furthermore, as skeletal muscle temperature declines, effective muscle contraction is affected, resulting in a progressive loss of shivering, muscle strength and muscle coordination. Shivering is capable of producing up to 500% more heat than normal, but when the muscles themselves get too cold to shiver effectively (at around a core temperature of 86-88 degrees F), the rate of onset of hypothermia increases. Furthermore, any medical or metabolic problem that impairs shivering thermogenesis (e.g, malnutrition, hypoglycemia, hypothyroidism, etc.) will hasten the onset of hypothermia. In addition, muscle cramping can occur during intense shivering, not only causing pain, but also adversely impacting motor control and mobility.

Core temperatures of around 93 degrees F are often associated with impaired judgement, difficulty in speaking, and slowed mentation. Further declines in core temperature to around 91 degrees F are associated with loss of motor control, continuing mental depression, a slowing heart rate and respiratory rate, and a cold-induced increase in urine production, thus increasing the risks of dehydration and further disrupting the body's metabolic defenses. Consciousness is usually lost at core temperatures of 82-86 degrees F.

At core temperatures around 89-90 degrees F, patients have an increased risk of cardiac dysrhythmias. These latter are probable at core temperatures around 86 degrees F. Spontaneous ventricular fibrillation or other potentially fatal dysrhythmias become increasingly likely as the heart temperature continues to decline. This is particularly true for core temperatures below 82-83 degrees F. However, even before that temperature, rough handling of a patient or even just moving a patient onto a litter has been known to precipitate cardiac arrest in the cold heart.

Shivering usually ceases around 86-88 degrees F, and with it, the body's primary defense against hypothermia. The body's oxygen consumption decreases progressively as the body cools. At a core temperature of around 90 degrees F, oxygen consumption is decreased by 25%. At a core temperature of around 82 degrees F, oxygen consumption is decreased by 50%. This decreased metabolism is associated with one positive benefit: the body is able to tolerate a reduced oxygen supply *(hypoxia) or even absent oxygen supply (e.g. cardiopulmonary arrest). Hypothermic patients who go into cardiac arrest have a longer period of time during which they can be successfully resuscitated since the cold brain and the cold heart are more resistant to irreversible damage from lack of oxygen. The colder the tissues at the time of cardiac arrest, the greater is the tolerance to anoxia. In contrast, cardiac arrest occurring in normothermic patients almost always leads to irreversible damage in four to six minutes and an inability to resuscitate them.*

The rate of onset of hypothermia can affect certain of the signs and symptoms observed or measured in the patient. Acute hypothermia (e.g., rapid onset, as in immersion into cold water) is often associated with an elevation in blood glucose levels. This is because immersion in cold water elicits an adrenalin response, which stimulates the outpouring of glucose into the blood. Chronic hypothermia (e.g., slow onset hypothermia developing over many hours) however, can be associated with low blood glucose levels, as periods of prolonged shivering deplete the body's energy supply (glycogen).

Regarding Mr. Fitzgerald's survival time during the interval between his last known telephone contact and when he was found unconscious in South Leigh Canyon, the Cold Exposure Survival Model (CESM), used for over 10 years by both the U.S. Coast Guard and Canadian Coast Guard, is helpful. This model, based on data from both human subject experiments (some of which I myself performed) in cold air and in cold water and on thermal manikin data in cold air and cold water, predicts an approximate time to unconsciousness (at a core temperature of 84-86 degrees F) given various survival parameters including the victim's gender, height, weight, age, clothing and environmental conditions of air temperature, wind, water temperature and (if the victim is immersed in water) the percentage of body immersion and the sea-state. Time to unconsciousness in a water survival situation is usually synonymous with death from drowning, unless the victim is totally out of the water. In land survival situations, unconsciousness is not usually synonymous with death, since cardia arrest occurs at lower body core temperatures than does loss of consciousness. The CESM algorithm thus predicts survival time to a core temperature of 84-86 degrees F.

Using the two lower body weights for Mr. Fitzgerald, listed above (120 and 135 lbs.), air temperatures from 10-20 degrees F, winds calm to light, and clothing to include a heavy parka, t-shirt, long sleeved shirt and light vest or shell (with clothing being wet), the following survival times are predicted (starting from Mr. Fitzgerald's last communication at 1943 hours on 19 January 2010:

135 lbs.: 6.9 to 13.4 hours (the lower number correlating to an air temperature of 10 degrees F with light winds, and the higher number correlating to an air temperature of 20 degrees F and calm winds).

120 lbs.: 6.2 to 12 hours (the lower number correlating to an air temperature of 10 degrees F with light winds, and the higher number correlating to an air temperature of 20 degrees F and calm winds).

It is thus my opinion that, to a reasonable degree of medical certainty, had Mr. Fitzgerald been rescued in the early morning hours of 20 January 2010, he would, more likely than not, have been alive and conscious at the time of rescue. Furthermore, his chances of successful resuscitation would have been, more likely than not, significantly improved had he been rescued prior to suffering hypothermia-induced cardio-pulmonary arrest."

* * *

Don Oscar woke around five in the morning. He had slept fairly well, considering he had stayed up later than usual. He didn't know why the Idaho people, and the Targhee ski patrol, had even bothered to try and find that lost skier at night. He was confident that as soon as they flew over in the heli they would spot him. That is, if he hadn't walked out, by himself, by this time. But Oscar hadn't received any call from dispatch reporting that the skier had walked out, so he was ready to proceed with the heli plan.

Oscar ambled into the kitchen and began to prepare his morning coffee. He glanced out the window; daylight wouldn't be making its presence felt for another few hours. He looked at his calendar to see what needed to be done today, Wednesday. Oh, that's right, he would have to call that rock climbing place. His son wanted to take a course. It would be a present for his 13th birthday. He could probably find a moment to call and sign him up for the course during a lull in the rescue operation.

Ah yes—the rescue operation. Oscar planned to take careful notes on the timing of today's rescue. Take off, first sighting, landing, pickup. It was possible the whole thing could be finished within a couple of hours. Of course, if the MP had frostbite, which was quite likely, they would have to drop him off at the hospital. Still, that wouldn't take too long.

Helicopter missions always put Oscar in a good mood. There was nothing in this world like flying in the mountains with an experienced pilot like Len Jameson, on a rescue mission to help someone. At 5:20 Oscar dialed Jameson on his cell. Len confirmed that he would be ready to meet Oscar at the heli hangar by 7:30 a.m. After hanging up, Oscar dialed the Jackson Sheriff's Office to let them know the search would resume at first light when he, Jameson and Clay Striver would be taking the ship up. He then dialed Tom Catalin. Oscar would have preferred not to. He had been a bit annoyed that Catalin had tried to argue with him last night, saying they ought to be doing a ground search. But Oscar was required to update him because Catalin was a senior board member of Search and Rescue. On the phone, Oscar informed him of his plan—that Oscar and heli pilot Jameson would be meeting at the hangar and take off at first light, weather permitting. Clay Striver would be there to meet them as well, to function as an additional spotter. Clay was the kind of person you always wanted to have with you in case anything went wrong. His Search and Rescue experience was invaluable, and he was experienced with avalanche conditions.

Oscar gritted his teeth when Catalin told him again they should have done a ground search. Well, he'd show Catalin. A couple hours from now, they would spot the MP, they'd collect the guy, and then Oscar would remind Catalin how much money had been saved by avoiding a futile nighttime search.

Oscar dialed Clay to make sure he was on his way to the hangar. Clay confirmed he would be there before first light.

He knew he had to speak with Terry Diamond so he called the Idaho Sheriff's Office. Diamond wasn't there so he told them he would try Terry's cell. Before he could do so, his phone rang; it was Len Jameson with a report on the weather forecast. Fog was likely, so they might have to wait a bit after first light. Still, they would meet at the hangar as planned and wait for suitable conditions. Most likely it would clear up enough to fly.

He dialed Terry Diamond. "Terry. Don."

"Hi Don. What are you, uh, do you want Idaho SAR to assist with the rescue?"

"Terry, listen. We'll be going up in the heli to pluck him out of there. You can be backup. Stage at Targhee with your team at 7:30, that should be good."

"Okay Don," Terry replied. "But do you think maybe we should stage down at the bottom of the canyon? You know, in case, uh, in case we need an ambulance or something? I mean, I hope not, but you know..."

"Yeah, look, don't worry about it," said Oscar impatiently. He really couldn't stand it when Terry rambled. The man never could get straight to the point!

"We're just going to pluck him right out," he continued. "If he's got frostbite we'll fly him to St. Johns. You guys are just backup, you understand? But keep me posted if you hear anything relevant from dispatch."

Oscar hung up and went to pour some coffee. The coffee smelled good. Carol always used to compliment him on his coffee.

But it had been a long time since she had complimented him on anything. Lately she had been so, well, silent. He tried to avoid thinking about it, but in his heart he knew she would be leaving him soon. What would happen if they split up? Maybe the first thing she'd miss about him would be his coffee. He wondered if she would still use the things he had given her over the years. If they split up, would she still wear that beige outfit he had bought her for her birthday? She looked great in that. He still wasn't sure if it was his fault or not. He couldn't recall having done anything really terrible, but somehow, things had just deteriorated over time. Well. No sense in going over it and over it. As long as he could see Junior, he could handle it.

Junior, though, seemed to favor his mother over his father. Whenever he needed help with his homework, or had some problem with his soccer coach, or one of his teammates, he went to Carol. Don tried his best to get Junior to open up to him, but the boy seemed almost afraid of him. Don couldn't imagine why. He had never hit the boy—well, except for that one time, when Junior was ten and he had stolen a comic book from the grocery store. But that had been almost three years ago.

The fact was, Don Oscar didn't like children much. Even his own son seemed foreign to him, and Don had never felt a bond with him even though the boy was his own flesh and blood. But he tried hard. He bought Junior most of the things he asked for. Don would sign him up for that rock climbing class today.

Oscar poured the fresh coffee into his favorite Miami Dolphins mug. He wasn't particularly a Dolphins fan, but he liked the mug. He took a few sips then placed the mug on the counter while he looked through his notes for a description of the MP, and realized he didn't have one. He would certainly need a description of clothing and so forth. Crap. He would have to call that ski group leader. Diamond had said last night that the ski group was still staying at the Parkway Inn in Jackson. Oscar went into his office to get the white pages and brought it back to the living room with his coffee. He found the number of the Parkway Inn and stored it in his phone. Then he jumped in the shower, got dressed, and poured another cup of coffee.

He wanted to be sure of the avalanche forecast. He searched in Contacts for the number and called. Avalanche forecast was "low." That was good. Now for that clothing description. Oscar hadn't spoken with the tour group leader the night before; he had left that task up to Terry Diamond. But since he himself was about to conduct the heli search, he knew he ought to get the information firsthand.

He called the Parkway Inn and spoke with the girl at the front desk. He asked to be connected with—he held the sheet of paper closer to his face—Ted Knowington, the ski group leader. "Ted Knowlton," the girl corrected him. She took Oscar's number, then she mentioned that several of the ski group people had spent most of the night hanging around the lobby, hoping that their friend would show up or that there would be some word from the Sheriff or Search and Rescue.

"Tell them not to worry," said Oscar. "We've got it under control."

Oscar was transferred to Ted's room, and Oscar spoke with him, advised him of the plan to do a helicopter search at first light. Ted gave Oscar a clothing description. He sounded relieved. He, too, mentioned that some of the ski group had stayed up all night long hoping Eddie would show up. Don wrote notes on the pad as Ted talked. What was the guy's last name? Oh yes, Fitzgerald.

From Oscar's personal notes, Deposition Exhibit 39A: "Called tour leader 'Ted' for clothing description also info about behavior. Said that he was a quiet person/loner not overly social would have dinner with other people on tour but would go back to room after. Good shape, Red Jacket, black pants, black hat. yellow ski goggles."

Oscar hung up, fooled around with his new phone for awhile, then received a call from the Jackson Sheriff's Office. A deputy wanted details of the heli search plan, which Oscar gave him. At 7:19 his phone rang again.

"Hello, Don? Jon Alexander, Targhee Ski Patrol."

"Hi Jon."

"Yeah, listen, I just wanted to double check I had this right—did you tell the Idaho team to stage at Targhee?"

"Yeah," replied Don in a gruff voice. "That's right."

"Well, we already have patrollers on duty at Targhee. The Idaho team isn't needed there. And as you know, last night we found the MP's tracks heading down the chute towards South Leigh. So, why don't we have Idaho stage down by the trailhead? They could be useful there if you need help."

Oscar couldn't believe the nerve of this guy. Hadn't he told them to stand down the night before? The incident was being handled by Wyoming Search and Rescue now. Case closed.

"Yeah, look Jon, the Idaho team is just backup, we don't need them," said Oscar. "We're gonna pluck the guy out of there and drop him off at St. Johns if he's got frostbite. That's it."

"You're assuming the MP will be mobile," said Jon. "We don't know that for sure."

"I've done hundreds of searches Jon. I think I know what I'm doing."

"Look Don, I don't mean to question your command. I'm just saying we are already covered at Targhee."

Oscar felt like hanging up on him. "I think you're worrying for no reason," he said. "Just let us handle it, okay?"

"If you don't want to work together on this, I understand," said Jon. "Or, actually, I don't understand. But again, my patrol team is on duty at Targhee, so I'm just offering you our assistance if you need it. That's all."

"Fine, fine," said Oscar. "If I need you, I've got your number here in my phone."

"Okay," said Jon. "Bye, then."

Oscar hung up. Some of these ski patrollers were a little full of themselves—just because they knew a thing or two about skiing didn't make them Search and Rescue experts. He took a sip of coffee and sat down on his living room sofa to look over his notes. Okay—red jacket, black pants & gloves, yellow goggles. With that red jacket the MP should be easy to spot from the air, Oscar thought. He could hardly wait to have another successful rescue under Wyoming SAR's belt to justify the cost of the new hangar.

It was hard to believe, but some of those idiots on the county board had actually argued with him against Wyoming SAR having their own helicopter hangar! "You can continue using the one at the airport," they said. "Or you can use privately-owned helicopters, the way you've done it with Harrison Ford." Oscar like the actor. He was a member of Teton County Wyoming SAR and had volunteered for missions in the past, supplying and piloting his own heli. But what if the guy was out shooting a movie or something? He was a popular actor, he couldn't be counted on to be available whenever you needed him. Anyway, an outfit with the stature of TCWSAR needed its own helicopter hangar, period.

He had the spiel memorized, he had to say it so often: Helicopters need to land in close proximity to the hangar in order to avoid spraying multi-million dollar private jets with ice and gravel from the heli blades. Fueling is also a big concern. The TCSAR helicopter needs to be stored with minimum fuel to be mission-ready for high altitude/close proximity rescues. The first priority for fueling at the Jackson airport is the commercial aircraft. Often SAR has to wait 45 minutes or longer to obtain fuel, greatly increasing the response time to an emergency where every minute matters. By adding a heliport to the new Search and Rescue building, SAR will be able to lower response times.

Some of the funds for the new Search and Rescue building had been raised already, through grants, private contributions, and the State of Wyoming. A meeting with the County administration was scheduled for the following week. Oscar looked forward to using today's successful mission to bolster his argument about the effectiveness of using helicopters in rescue situations. It was faster and more effective than boots on the ground when trying to find a missing person on the mountain.

Oscar allowed himself to reflect for a moment: over the past fifteen years he had built this organization up from practically nothing. He wasn't trying to take all of the credit—a lot of people had contributed to the operation and success of the team—but let's face it, before he got here there wasn't anything happening, not really. So if he was a little bit territorial about it, well, he had a right to be, goddam it. Search and Rescue is serious business. You can't have yahoos on snowmobiles running up and down the mountain thinking they know how to conduct a proper search, not to mention a rescue operation. Christ. Well, he would just have to continue to find ways to keep the flame burning under the county on this helicopter issue. Pretty soon they would be thanking him, saying "Why did we wait so long to do this?" It might take a while, but he could wait.

* * *

Rich tried to close the room door quietly so as not to wake up Cheryl. They had been out late last night, celebrating his birthday, just the two of them. He was in a good mood. He felt so lucky to have someone like her. They had so much in common, and she enjoyed skiing almost as much as he did. But he didn't think she'd be going out to the mountain today. She had been sucking down those Advils yesterday, topping them off with several glasses of vino during dinner. She loved to ski, but she didn't train during the off season the way he did. So she would typically overdo it the first couple days and need to take some time off in the middle of the trip to recuperate. But that was okay, she could go shopping or sit around and relax, while he might go out with Ross and Marco, or maybe Fred, or whoever. Rich pocketed his key and went downstairs to the breakfast room.

There were several people already there. Rich immediately noticed that the mood of the group was not as boisterous and upbeat as usual. Something was definitely wrong.

"Hey, Marco. What's up?" Marco was drinking coffee, standing by the sideboard in the lobby outside of the breakfast room.

"You haven't heard about Eddie, have you?" was the response.

"What? Eddie Cola? What about him?"

"We don't know. He's missing. Never came back from Targhee yesterday."

Rich squinted, worry lines appearing on his forehead. "What are you talking about? Wasn't he on the bus with us?"

Marco put his cup down on the sideboard and started buttering a bagel slice. It wasn't a New York bagel, but it would have to do. "Well, going there, he was on the bus, and coming back, he wasn't on the bus. Nobody noticed until we got back here, and people were going out to dinner, and that guy J.R. who's his roommate noticed Eddie's skis weren't in the room. Most of us have been up all night, waiting for word from Search and Rescue." He took a bite of bagel and looked at Rich accusingly. "We were looking for you guys, where were you?"

"Shit. Shit. I had no idea. We went out to dinner by ourselves to celebrate my birthday."

"Happy birthday, man."

"Yell, well, I guess it's not so happy now. So are people out looking for Eddie or what?"

Marco took another bite of his bagel. "They searched for him last night, and it got too late and they called it off. I guess they're gonna keep searching again today."

"I wouldn't want to spend the night outside in the cold around here," said Rich. "You could get frostbite."

The two men were silent for a moment. Rich saw a few others in the breakfast room, voices low, probably having similar conversations.

"This is unbelievable. Do you think something happened to him, like he broke his leg or something?"

Marco shrugged. "Who knows. It happened to Mario. This really sucks. Eddie's a good skier. I don't know where he was skiing, but you know Cola, he doesn't duck ropes so he had to be on one of the regular trails. 'Course the visibility wasn't great, so some of us are thinking maybe he skied out of bounds by accident."

"Probably he did. Because Targhee isn't that big. If they were searching the resort grounds, they would have found him if he was in bounds." Rich poured a cup of coffee from the large thermos into a Styrofoam cup and snapped a lid on it so he could take it back to the room. "I better go tell Cheryl. She's gonna be really upset."

"Okay. You going out today?"

"Yeah, I'll be back down." Rich went upstairs. He carefully placed the coffee cup down on the carpet while he searched for which pocket had the key, then opened the door to the room. Cheryl was still sleeping. He sat down next to her on the edge of the bed, putting the coffee on the nightstand next to the clock radio. "Honey? Honey, wake up." His wife stirred in her sleep. He gently stroked her arm, and she opened her eyes.

"Ohhhhh, what time is it?"

"It's early. Honey, I just got some bad news."

Cheryl sat up in the bed, pulling the covers up around her. "What? What's wrong?"

Rich motioned to the coffee cup, still steaming in the cold January morning. They both liked to sleep in a cold room so they had the heat down low. "I brought you some coffee. I don't think you're going to want to go back to sleep. I talked to Marco downstairs. He said that Eddie, Eddie Cola, he never came back to the hotel last night. They think he got lost at Targhee. Search and Rescue's been out looking for him but apparently they haven't found him yet."

"What!" Cheryl rubbed her eyes, fully awake now. "Eddie is lost? Are you sure? Are you sure he's not here?"

"Yes," Rich said. "His skis aren't here and neither is he."

"How could someone get lost at Targhee? Anyway, I'm sure he was on the bus with us," Cheryl protested. "Wasn't he? Wasn't he with us on the big bus while the van went to pick up Mario at the hospital?"

"Well, that's what I thought too, but apparently he was not on either of the buses coming back. Eddie's so quiet, no one noticed, I guess."

"But doesn't Fred always do a head count to make sure everyone is there?"

"I'm sure he does, but remember how confusing it was, everyone was changing seats and loading their gear on the big bus to make room for Mario in the van. So maybe Fred miscounted. That's probably what happened."

"Oh no, this is terrible!" Cheryl got up and quickly put on the same clothes she had worn the night before. "Let me get dressed, I have to go downstairs and find out what's going on."

"Okay," Rich said. "But some people still plan to go skiing, so I'll probably go snowboarding with Ross and Marco. Can you call my cell and let me know what's going on? 'Cause you're not going to ski, right?"

"What!" she exclaimed. "Eddie Cola is missing, and you're going to go snowboarding?"

"Well honey," Rich said defensively, "there's nothing we can do about it. We just have to wait for word from the authorities."

"I can't believe it! Our friend is out there lost in the freezing cold and you don't even seem to care!"

"Cheryl, don't be ridiculous, of course I care. It's just that we came all this way to go snowboarding and skiing and, well, I want to go."

"I never thought you could be this callous. I'm really shocked, Richard."

Rich threw a pillow from the bed at the chair in the corner of the room. "Cheryl, what do you expect me to do? Sit around and bite my nails till he gets found? Jesus!"

"Okay then! You go out by yourself. I'm going downstairs to wait for Eddie!" She went into the bathroom and slammed the door. He heard her crying, and the toilet flushing.

"Jesus Christ," muttered Rich. He grabbed his gear bag and left the room.

* * *

Jon Alexander was lying in bed, awake, at 6:30 a.m. in a room at Targhee's main lodge, where he had spent the remaining hours of darkness after the frustration of last night when the search had been called off. He had slept poorly, despite being dog tired after working all day and then directing a search till after midnight. He should have slept like a log. But no. It bothered him that Don Oscar had called off the search without even being on scene. It bothered him that there had been no boots on the ground from Wyoming. Zero. None. All Oscar had done was make a few phone calls, sit back and let Targhee Ski Patrol and Teton County Idaho SAR do all the work. Then they planned to swoop down and make a dramatic rescue in the helicopter, like a fricking' vulture grabbing its prize after some other animal kills it.

Jon got up and unplugged his cellphone from its charger. He was only the Acting Director of Ski Patrol while Director Pete Kerry was out of town; he needed to keep Pete in the loop so he called his cell and left a message. Then he dialed the head of Targhee, General Manager Brett Montague, to let him know that a day skier had gone out of bounds and become lost, necessitating a search. Again, he was only able to leave a message. He began to dial Jesse, who had also stayed the night at Targhee rather than making the trip back to Driggs. Jesse beat him to it.

"Jon. Terry just paged out Idaho SAR to stage at Targhee, you know that?" Jesse's voice sounded unusually low and gravelly; he probably had slept like crap too.

"What's wrong with those guys?" asked Jon. "That's nuts— we know Edward is in South Leigh Canyon! That's where Idaho should stage. Then if Wyoming needs any help on scene, the Idaho team can assist."

"Yeah, that's what I was thinking, but I called Terry and he told me those were Wyoming's orders. It's a Wyoming search."

"Damn it! Pisses me off, you know?" said Jon. "And what, Wyoming isn't going to bother to page their own team today either? I'm going to call Don Oscar and see what he's thinking—if anything. I'll call you back."

Jon disconnected and decided to take a quick shower before dialing Oscar. It would give him some time to cool off and plan his conversation in a way that wouldn't set off the volatile Wyoming Search and Rescue coordinator. After a short shower, Jon got back on the phone to see why Oscar had directed Idaho to stage at Targhee, which seemed pointless. When he got Oscar on the phone, Jon suggested to him that Idaho SAR would potentially be more useful staging at South Leigh, in case there was a medical issue or some other problem extracting the lost skier. Oscar was his usual cantankerous self, insisting that Idaho SAR was just backup and that the decision had been made for them to stage at Targhee. Not wanting to waste time arguing, Jon signed off. He wanted to get over to the mountain. Cathy was on Early Bird shift today, so the two of them could ski down to Rick's and then to the North Boundary. From the ground, they could signal to the helicopter where the tracks exited the resort, in case they couldn't be seen from the air. He went back into the bathroom and glanced in the mirror. Even after the shower he looked like hell, but there was no time for personal grooming now.

* * *

The Teton County Idaho Sheriff's office 911 dispatch room was nice and warm. The computers and console equipment added a few more degrees, and Sharon Courier was grateful for it on these freezing January mornings. She had been on duty all night, and had listened to the 911 calls from the lost skier over and over. It was now after 7 in the morning and she was listening to them again. There was something odd about the skier's voice—it sounded as if his speech was a bit slurred, or that perhaps he had an unusual way of speaking. It wasn't like a retarded person, exactly, but it had a quality somewhat similar to that. Sort of stilted, or unnatural. She kept going back over the calls, occasionally adding her new observations to the dispatch log.

Sharon looked up when Tesha Wilson walked in, bundled up in matching pink hat, gloves and scarf. Tesha waved hello and quickly took off her winter armor, hanging it on the wall pegs in the corner of the room. "What's going on, Sharon?" she asked.

"There's been a search on for a lost skier from Targhee," Sharon replied. "He called in a few times last night. He didn't have good cell reception so the calls kept getting disconnected."

She continued to fill in Tesha on the details of the search, as far as she knew them.

One might think the 911 dispatcher would know everything that was going on, but that wasn't so. They joked with one another about being on a need-to-know basis as far as Search and Rescue was concerned. Once a search was underway, the 911 dispatchers were in the dark unless the SAR people needed some additional information or assistance.

"They called off the search last night around midnight," Sharon continued. "They're supposed to resume this morning. Wyoming SAR is taking their helicopter out to South Leigh Canyon to look for him."

"Why ever did they call off the search?" Tesha asked. "It was dangerously cold out there last night—I mean, maybe we're more used to it out here—but the lost guy is from back East, you said?"

"Yeah. New York. Well, all I know is, they decided to stop and wait till morning to pick him up. But Targhee Ski Patrol had found his tracks last night, and they basically knew where he was."

"If they knew where he was, why didn't the Search and Rescue people go get him last night then?" Tesha shook her head and went over to the coffee machine.

"There was something, some issue with Wyoming," said Sharon. "I heard Terry talking to them on the phone. Like, Wyoming said okay, you guys are done, we're taking over. They said they planned to take the helicopter out this morning."

"You know how boys are," said Tesha, "they love to play with their expensive toys." She took a sip of coffee and sat down at the console next to Sharon. "Anything else I should know before I start?" she asked.

"Yeah. You know, I've been listening to the skier's 911 calls all night. They're a little garbled. I wish Mark had asked Viola to access the Eventide system."

"I agree, the calls are a lot easier to hear on the Eventide," said Tesha, referring to the superior 911 recording system that was locked in a separate room. "It's too bad we're not allowed to use it all the time. But after the meeting last night, Viola told me she was going home. So she could easily have come back over here and checked it, if Mark had asked her."

"When I came in for my shift, he acted like he got everything," said Sharon. "Could you listen to these calls? Because I'm definitely hearing some stuff he didn't write down in the log."

"Okay," said Tesha, sitting down at the console in the chair Sharon had vacated. She drew the log book closer to her and looked at Sharon's last entry, made at 7:16 a.m.: "Ed also says he is near a stream with fallen trees."

* * *

The three of them stood outside the hangar at the Jackson Hole airport looking up at the sky. "Looks like it's going to clear any minute," Jameson, the pilot, said. "Let's go up."

"Don," said Clay Striver, "You advised the Jackson Sheriff's office of the mission?"

"Yeah," said Don, "I spoke with the Deputy about forty five minutes ago. Terry is staging at Targhee just for backup. We're good."

At 7:56 a.m. they were airborne: Jameson piloting the Bell 407 helicopter with Don Oscar and Clay Striver on board.

"Don, are we flying directly to Leigh Canyon?" Jameson asked.

"Yeah. The MP has a red jacket, black pants and gloves, and yellow goggles."

Don Oscar's personal notes, Deposition Exhibit 39A: "Left airport with Clay Striver, myself, Len Jameson. Flew to LC [Leigh Canyon] found tracks going down chute/gully. Followed tracks to lone snowmobile track. Saw sidesteps going uphill. Followed these tracks to end of snowmobile track and realized the track went downhill on same track. Followed track downhill to where the snowmobile had crossed stream over small bridge. Track went downstream following stream on so. side. Track crossed stream at least 6 times, continued following track through trees and stream."

Jameson pressed the radio button. "This is Jackson helicopter 42 Mica Alpha, pilot Len Jameson."

The radio crackled. "42 Mica Alpha go ahead."

"We're off ground," said Jameson, "headed to Targhee via Teton Pass."

"Copy."

Clay Striver adjusted the focus on his binoculars, scanning the canyon as they began a series of wide circles over the area. He saw two skiers at the top of the chute at Rick's Basin—Don had advised him that would be Jon Alexander and another ski patroller from Targhee.

"There are the tracks," Clay said, pointing down to the chute, an open stretch lined by clusters of Douglas Firs.

"I see 'em," Don Oscar said. "Len, can you follow these down?"

Jameson guided the ship over the tracks, deftly manipulating the cyclic stick, collective lever, and anti-torque pedals of the aircraft.

"Look," said Oscar, pointing, "there's a snowmobile track."

"Got it," said Striver. "You see the sidestepping ski tracks on the hill there?"

"No."

"Look to the left of the snowmobile track."

"Okay, got it. Len, bring us over here so we can get a better look," Oscar directed the pilot.

The ship banked and approached the snowmobile track, reducing altitude slightly.

"The side steps and the snowmobile track are merged here," Striver remarked.

"Yeah. Look there, the snowmobile track ends."

Striver trained the binoculars on what seemed to be the end of the snowmobile track. "I see what happened," said Striver. "The skier was following the snowmobile track, then the snowmobile came down the same way. Let's go down further, toward the creek."

Jameson piloted the helicopter further north, in the direction of Leigh Creek. They passed over Rick's Basin, the cross country skiing area, and then approached the chute that Jared and Andrew had skied to the previous night. The chute descended another thousand feet to South Leigh Creek. Before the helicopter reached the creek, it had to pass over a thickly-treed area of Targhee National Forest. Oscar and Striver, binoculars in place, were focused on following the track as it wound through the forest. They approached the creek, winding its way through the wilderness in a northwest direction. They saw the snowmobile track crossed a small snow bridge over to the creek's opposite bank.

"Look," said Oscar, "the boot pack stays on the south side of the stream. Can you see it, Len?"

"Copy that," Jameson responded. "Following track on south side of stream."

"Keep following the track," said Oscar. "Okay, you see how he's crossing the stream, he's done it twice already."

"Right," Striver said. They counted four more crossings as they continued to follow the track.

"Jesus," said Oscar. "What's going on with this guy? Why does he keep crossing the creek?"

The repeated crossings indicated a lack of logic on the part of the skier. Perhaps, thought Oscar, he'd been affected by hypothermia and been unable to think clearly. Oscar felt an unpleasant gnawing in his gut; he began to doubt his decision to postpone the search till this morning.

"Hey, what's that," said Jameson, pointing out his side window. Oscar and Striver leaned over to look.

"Red jacket," said Oscar, "that's him."

"He's prone. No movement," said Striver.

"Shit," said Oscar. He noted the time: it was 8:37 a.m. "Len, land us on the snowmobile trail, Clay and I will skin in from there."

Located on the north side of South Leigh Creek, the unpaved road to which Oscar referred was used by hikers in the warmer months, and by snowmobilers during the winter. It was crusted over with hardened snow and ice, and Jameson skillfully landed the ship on it. Striver and Oscar disembarked with their skis, ducking under the propeller, and proceeded to gear up to reach Eddie.

"We'll have to cross the stream, what's the best way?" Oscar asked Striver, who pointed to a spot upstream from where they were standing.

Clay Striver: "We landed on the snowmobile trail, got out, put on our skis with skins... grabbed the packs... and went over to the creek, in four or five feet of snow now, and then steep banks on the creek. We tried to find the shallowest crossing. Even then it was over our ski boots. We crossed the creek, then we split up. Don went one way and I went the other way because we weren't sure exactly where —we had seen him from the sky, but now we're on the ground and we have to locate the subject. And so we skied one way or the other. I think Don found him going upstream."

Oscar had a portable AED—an Automated External Defibrillator— in his backpack. He had brought it along just in case. Unfortunately, it was looking like they might need to use it. Shit, why did the guy have to be passed out? He was supposed to be sitting on a rock, smoking a cigarette, feeling like a jerk while he waited for us, he thought. When they reached Eddie, who was lying like a corpse in the snow, Oscar felt another wave of anxiety.

Perhaps he'd been wrong, after all—maybe they should have continued the search last night.

Oscar's notes: "Found Edward face down in snow. Rolled Edward over. Edward was unconscious, unresponsive. Not breathing. No pulse detected. Started rescue breathing. Edward was very hypothermic. Called Dr. Steeler at St. Johns and was instructed to use AED to look for heart activity. Leads were placed on Edward and AED monitor showed a flat line although trying to call back out to Steeler AED noted some slight heart electrical activity. Sporatic [sic]. Steeler was again consulted and his order was to continue rescue breaths back to St. Johns although he first instructed us to try and call EIRMAC [Eastern Idaho to take Edward to Idaho Falls hospital. EIRMAC stated due to weather they could not respond. The decision was made to transport Edward to St. Johns.

Edward was packaged with heat packs/hypothermia bag placed on backboard strap [sic] in then placed on air mattress then evacuated through trees across stream and back to helicopter.

After dropping Clay & I off at scene, Ski Patrol was contacted (only radio communication) to assist with transport and additional medical personell [sic]. Two Targhee Ski Patrol were picked up at helispot at base of Ski Area and flown to scene.

Via radio Terry Diamond was contacted because of his paramedic medical training and was picked up at trailhead with helicopter and brought to scene.

* * *

Terry Diamond was exhausted. He had been up half the night dealing with the search for the Fitzgerald man, and in the end, after letting him do all the work, Don Oscar and Clay Striver forced him to stand down, insisting that they would take it from there. Okay, fine. It was politics, and Terry knew better than to get in the middle of it. He had stepped on some toes before, back in the day, and it hadn't been pretty. So if that's how Wyoming wanted to play it, the responsibility was on them.

He was at home on January 20th, relieved to have the morning off from SAR duties, when he got a phone call from the Idaho Sheriff's office asking him to report for duty. Evidently, Fish and Game and a couple of Idaho SAR folks were going to go on snowmobiles up the South Leigh Canyon road to assist Wyoming in the extraction of the lost skier, who had been found lying in the snow, unconscious.

Diamond was already on his way when he received a call on his cell, this time from Don Oscar. Well, well, well. It seems that old Don was in trouble! Seems he needed some medical personnel so he was calling good old Terry for some EMT assistance.

Oscar had a way of ordering you around even when he was asking for your help. Terry listened as he was directed to go to the winter parking area, about two miles past the state line into Wyoming, where the helicopter would pick him up and fly him to the scene.

Driving along the ramrod-straight Rt. 33 on the way to the canyon, he couldn't erase the rather unbecoming thoughts that sailed through his mind.

I am Don Oscar, the great and powerful!

Thanks Terry, we'll take it from here, huh?

We're just backup, huh?

Well, I guess I'm a little more than backup now, Don.

Diamond rolled down his window. He was feeling more awake now, but it seemed like another long day was in store. After this EMT run there would be reports to fill out... then he'd have to check in at the bail bonds office, his actual business. He rolled up the window again—it was cold out.

* * *

After a sleepless night, Mandy Jones rose around 8:30 a.m. She hadn't been able to stop thinking about Edward Fitzgerald. Where was he, what had happened to him? There really wasn't anyplace else besides South Leigh Canyon where he could have ended up. They knew it for sure after Andrew and Jared had found his tracks going down the gully.

When they had gone down to the canyon the night before, after the search had been suspended for the night, she and the boys had discussed the situation while driving toward the trailhead in Jared's car. None of them could understand why the search had been suddenly called off. They knew where the lost skier was, and at least they could have gone down to the canyon and driven up the road on snowmobiles. The three of them had even devised a hypothetical plan, whereby searchers with three snowmobiles would be deployed. The lead snowmobile would go all the way to the trailhead at the end of the road. The second one would go two thirds of the way, and the last, one third. They would cut their engines on arrival at their designated spots. Then they would shout and/or blow whistles to try to contact Edward. If he was conscious, he would most likely hear at least one person shouting for him and hopefully, he would be able to respond. Stage two would be traveling up the mountain on the snowmobiles. The team could communicate with each other via radio.

Unless the skier had gotten hung up on the way down the mountain, with a broken leg or some injury that rendered him immobile, he would most likely be down at the bottom of that chute, and within shouting distance of the road. Maybe he would even have reached the road by that time. In any case, it had seemed senseless to them that no one wanted to go down to the road and at least shout for him, even if they didn't enter the woods. So that's what the three young patrollers had done. There was no rule against that; Jon had said only that they couldn't use the snowmobiles.

"Why do you think Wyoming called it off?" Jared had asked, both hands on the wheel because of the slippery roads.

"Because they want to use their helicopter," Andrew had quickly replied. He was aware of Wyoming's helicopter story because he knew someone on the county board in Jackson. "They want to show off."

"Yes," said Jared, but when someone's in trouble, wouldn't you want to do everything possible? The helicopter can only be used in the day, and if the person is hypothermic or injured, they might not last until morning."

"I agree, Jared," said Mandy. "From what I understand, Edward made a few 911 calls and then stopped calling. What does that tell you?"

"It tells me that either his cell died," said Andrew, "or couldn't get a signal, or else he was incapacitated."

"And if he was incapacitated, he definitely needed to have people out looking for him, on the ground." said Jared.

"Well," said Mandy, "Maybe we'll find him, and he's okay. Let's hope so. Then we can call for an ambulance if needed. He might just be lost, and not know which direction to walk. He might be okay other than that."

"The only thing is," said Andrew, "In order for him to reach the road he would have to cross that creek."

"And if he had to cross the creek," continued Jared, "then he's wet."

"And if he's wet," finished Mandy, "he's in an advanced stage of hypothermia by now." She sighed.

Sitting on the edge of her bed, replaying this conversation in her mind, Mandy decided to call the Targhee ski patrol dispatcher at the summit of Fred's Mountain. It was her day off, but she wouldn't be able to do a thing without knowing what had happened to Edward.

She phoned summit dispatch and spoke with Gary Thibault, the Incident Investigation Supervisor. "Hi Gary, it's Mandy Jones from Ski Patrol. I just wanted to check on whether the MP from last night had been found yet or not."

She listened intently as Thibault replied, "Actually, he has been located and there's patrollers and SAR down there right now working on the extraction."

She shivered involuntarily. "So that means ... is he ...?"

"He's alive but unconscious."

"Oh no!"

"Listen, you were on dispatch for the search last night, right?" said Thibault.

"Yes."

"Okay. We're going to need you to come in and write a report. How soon can you get here?"

Mandy replied quickly, "I can be there by eleven."

"Okay, can we meet at base, I'll bring the report form."

"Yes, I'll be there."

"Thanks Mandy." He hung up.

So, she thought, placing the phone back on its cradle, *he's non-responsive. He might not make it, at this point. I was right. I told them all—Terry Diamond, Jon, Jesse—there was a risk of hypothermia, and they ignored me. If I were a guy, they would have listened to me! But they always act so macho, like women aren't capable of doing the same things men do. They're so holier-than-thou sometimes. They always assume people ski out of bounds on purpose just to get to the powder. No one takes into account that those "closed" signs are very sporadically placed, and in foggy conditions you can easily ski between two signs and not see either one. I'll bet that's exactly what happened to Edward. Because if he saw the signs, he would've stopped, or at least slowed down, to think about whether he was going to keep going for the powder. But it just doesn't sound like he was that type of skier. I'll bet he didn't see the signs.*

I know what I'll do... I'm going to join whoever's doing the NBT sweep, and check his tracks going out of bounds. Then I'll know from looking at the tracks whether he stopped or not. If he didn't stop, that means he just continued down the fall line thinking he was still on the trail!

* * *

Bill Redmond, a 31 year old ski patroller and EMT who had worked for Targhee since 2001, arrived at the resort around 8 a.m. and parked his car in his usual spot. He trudged through a bit of fresh snowfall the plow had missed as he stepped onto the curb on his way into the building.

Redmond had been out the previous evening and had left his cell phone at home, and had not received the message from Jon Alexander: "Bill—we have a potential lost skier, could you come up and help us out with this operation?"

He also hadn't checked his cell when he got home, late, but heard the message upon waking. He expected by now the situation had been resolved. When he reported for work, however, Jon Alexander immediately asked him to go take photos of the lost skier's tracks at the North Boundary Traverse. He had just finished doing this when he and Jesse O'Leary, who was doing a sweep elsewhere on the mountain, were both dispatched to respond to South Leigh Canyon via helicopter. They each proceeded directly to the area known as the Hamster Loop, where they boarded the ship at 8:51 a.m.

"Hey Jesse," said Bill as they fastened their seat belts. "I'm sorry, I didn't get the message about the search until this morning."

"Yeah. We had teams searching, but around midnight Wyoming said to stand down."

The noise of the helicopter filled the air and left no need for further conversation. Jesse looked out the window of the Bell 407 as they flew over the ridge of Fred's Mountain and began their descent toward South Leigh Canyon. *We should have gone in,* he thought. *We made a mistake. We knew he was down in the canyon, we should have ignored Wyoming's order and gone to get him. I could have urged Terry to authorize bringing the Idaho SAR snowmobiles down to the summer road. Why didn't I push for that? If the guy doesn't make it ... it will be partially my fault.*

The ship landed and Redmond and O'Leary disembarked, joining other members of the Idaho SAR team standing by. Personnel from the Idaho Dept. of Fish and Game had also been deployed to assist in the rescue operation. The Idaho SAR and the Fish and Game folks remained near the helicopter while Redmond and O'Leary proceeded downslope on skis, descending the road cut and crossing a terrace. They descended again and crossed another terraced section of terrain. They continued on their skis, crossing a somewhat flat section to the edge of South Leigh Creek. Scouting for a good place to cross the creek, they decided on a spot. Removing their skis and carrying them, Redmond and O'Leary forded the creek through a densely treed area.

Redmond: "*I think there were spots that I jumped over that were probably up to a foot and a half in depth. I think probably where my feet actually touched down scouting for the driest way to cross maybe eight inches, a foot depth, and then probably 40 feet across... my skis were already off because I had to take them off to cross the creek, and so I was already on foot. And because it was uphill out of the creek I decided it was best to just continue carrying my skis at that point and deal with the downfall and the forest, it was probably the most efficient means of travel in that direction, on foot.*"

On the other side of the creek, with water in their ski boots, Redmond and O'Leary approached Oscar and Striver standing next to Eddie's supine body lying in the snow about 200 feet to the northeast. Eddie was still in the spot Oscar and Striver had found him, although they had rolled him over to assess his airway.

Redmond estimated that the total distance from where they landed the helicopter to the point where Eddie was found was about five hundred yards. He looked down at Eddie and saw his skin color was pale and frozen-looking. **Redmond: "He appeared dead, but we proceeded as if he was severely hypothermic."** Redmond also noticed Eddie's ski jacket and pants were older models, not the latest equipment. Eddie's left hand was gloved, but the right was not. The missing glove was not immediately visible.

Redmond knelt down behind Eddie's head, preparing to create a suction seal on the patient's mouth with a medical device known as a bag valve mask. The device enables a rescuer to deliver rescue breaths to the patient efficiently and hygienically. One breath is delivered every five seconds. Redmond disconnected the AED monitor that Oscar had brought, and attached the more advanced model he had with him. The AED was attached using pads placed on the patient's heart, shoulder, and torso, near the kidneys. The AED's automation indicated it was analyzing the heart rate. If advised, a shock would be administered from the heart pad, however the machine reported an "unshockable rhythm," so none was delivered. This was the same reading that Don Oscar and Clay Striver had gotten before Redmond and O'Leary had arrived.

Don Oscar turned his head to the sound of cracking twigs and the crunch of boots on the hardening snow. He watched Terry Diamond approach; he felt relieved that there were now medical personnel on hand to deal with this situation.

"You found him right here?" asked Terry.

"Yeah," Oscar replied. "We just rolled him over. We're getting 'unshockable rhythm' off the AED."

Diamond knelt in the snow and began to examine the patient. He turned and leveled his gaze on Don Oscar's face. "Looks like we might be too late." Oscar looked away and was silent.

Redmond: "*Other Idaho SAR personnel arrived and we packaged the patient and transported him to the helicopter. . . Once piece of equipment was a litter designed for snow. And we packaged Mr. Fitzgerald into the litter. And we set up webbing, which is rope material to drag, additional rescuers help drag the patient to the near edge of the creek. We scouted, took us a little while, scouted a safe way to cross the creek. And then we at that time picked up the litter and managed to carry the litter across the creed. Which proved slightly challenging due to the rocky, bouldery, slippery nature in ski boots... There were other Search and Rescue members that helped us out. It would have been very difficult for just the four of us to manage it... in the meantime there were Search and Rescue members trying to punch in a snowmobile track as close to the other side of the creek as possible, which was not very close . . They were able to make a loop. So that's what they were kind of working on, improving the extraction route beyond... We then loaded the patient in the helicopter with the two Wyoming SAR team members [Oscar and Striver]. The helicopter took off to Jackson. . . We went back across the creek to gather all the remaining gear and ski equipment and shuttled it back across the creek and up the boot pack to the snowmobile track and back to the road. And packed all that gear into the Idaho Search and Rescue transportation sleds, snowmobiles. I rode out on a sled behind a snowmachine... From the winter trailhead, [an] Idaho Search and Rescue member, whose name I can't recall, gave us a ride to our houses. Then after grabbing food and clean dry clothes I believe I carpooled up with Jesse because I didn't [have] my car, [it] was still at Targhee.*"

* * *

Mandy sat at a desk in a small room at Grand Targhee Resort, surrounded by boxes of office supplies. She began to fill out the report form that Gary Thibault had given her. *I don't care if my statement doesn't go over well. I'm going to say what I really think.*

Transcript of Mandy Jones' First Handwritten Report on the Ski Patrol Search of January 19, 2010. (She was Later Asked to Revise and Re-Submit Her Report):

"At 8:30 p.m. I was having dinner w/ Jared & Andrew & Cathy when Jon A. called and asked that 2-3 patrollers respond back up to Targhee for a reported missing person. I volunteered to go w/ Andrew & Jared as I happened to have my gear in my car. We had little info regarding the missing party (MP). Upon arrival we were met by Clark (Security) who informed us he had sent 2 groomers out N. to reported area.

Patrollers were breifed [sic] by Jon A. about 911 call made by the MP and given assignments: Jon & Jesse on snowmos, one to head to reported tracks out of bounds & one to Rick's Basin as MP reported last riding an 'old 2 person chair and ending up in an aspen meadow'. Jared & Andrew were assigned to standby and I was tasked as dispatch & recorder.

I was to record all radio transmissions, answer incoming calls and update the 3 [Idaho] SAR members upon their arrival.

I recorded the departure, arrival, findings & transmissions of each team that was out. I also recorded the description of the MP and profile along with the communications I had w/ Terry Diamond. Please review the 3 pgs. of notes attached, for times, events and specific details.

As a new patroller @ GT and new to Teton Valley I do not know the topography of this out of bounds area well but felt that reports of this particular area, and knowing what I do of this area in conjunction with the MP's profile felt like we were facing a serious situation. [undecipherable word] sending Jared & Andrew out to follow suspected ski tracks they confirmed the skier had taken off his skis, dragging them and continued down toward S. Leigh Canyon. I felt that Jon A. did an excellent job communicating with Jared & Andrew and clearly described at what location he wanted them to stop as there was a concern for their safety in avalanche terrain outside of GT's controlled boundaries.

At the point it was confirmed that the MP was outside of GT's juricdiction [sic] and unsafe for patrol to continue—there was a 3 way conference call btwn. Terry Diamond, Don Oscar and Jesse O'Leary to determin [sic] what could be done from the bottom entrance of S. Leigh, up canyon. All 3 SAR members & myself were present. The outcome seemed to be that no further effort would be made until daybreak. Jack Stills expressed that staging an ambulance @ S. Leigh and sending 2 snowmachines up canyon on the snowmo road would possibly be worthwhile. This idea was rejected by Jesse O'Leary and the others in charge of JH SAR and Teton County SAR. I was not clear on why this idea was rejected and while I cannot say if reaching the MP from up canyon would have provided a different outcome—I would have at least felt like everything possible was done that could have, unfortantly [sic] given the outcome I don't feel that all safe possible options were explored and do not feel like the situation was taken as seriously as it could have been."

* * *

Shortly after lunchtime Deputy Dammer pulled into the parking lot of the Parkway Inn, not looking forward to the conversation she was about to have. When she entered the lobby she found it was empty save for Mackenzie, the owner's daughter, behind the front desk. The young girl looked up eagerly when the deputy came in. "Oh, Deputy—have they found him?"

"Yes, he's been found," replied Dammer. "I need to speak with the tour leader, is he here?"

"Oh thank God!" said Mackenzie. She gestured toward her right, where soft conversation was emanating from the little room where Eddie had eaten breakfast with the ski group just the day before. "They're in there," said Mackenzie. "Is he okay?"

Dammer strode into the breakfast room without answering. Fred and Ted were the only ones there, drinking coffee. They both rose when Dammer came in.

"Deputy, what's going on?" asked Ted.

"Let's sit down," the deputy responded. They seated themselves and the men looked expectantly at her.

"Edward has been found," she said, "but the news is not good, I'm afraid. He was down at the bottom of South Leigh Canyon, but he was unconscious. He's been evacuated to St. John's Medical Center, here in Jackson. He's alive, but—"

"But what?" said Fred, "but what?"

"His heartbeat is very faint. It's possible he may not be able to be resuscitated." She shook her head.

"What!" exclaimed Fred. "I don't understand! Was he hurt? Why was he unconscious for Christ sake?"

Dammer instinctively rested her right hand on her firearm strapped to her belt. "Please, Mr. McKuen, I understand your frustration, I feel the same way. I really don't know exactly what happened yet, probably no one does. Apparently his clothes were frozen on his body, indicating that he probably fell into the creek at a certain point during the night. That would explain how he became severely hypothermic—"

"Hypothermic, what's that," demanded Fred.

"It basically means that you're freezing to death, Fred," said Ted. "It's when your body temperature becomes too low to function."

"Yes, exactly," said Dammer, grateful for his jumping in.

"Oh, Eddie! Eddie, Eddie!" cried Fred, putting his head in his hands. He broke into sobs. "Eddie, no, no, no, no, no..."

"Fred, take it easy," said Ted, putting a hand on his shoulder. "There's still a chance he's gonna make it. Right, Deputy?"

Dammer looked at Ted, her lips tightening. "Yes, of course there's still a chance. If it's possible, then they'll be able to do it. It's just that... " She paused, unsure of how to put it. "It's just that, you need to be prepared for, for, if he doesn't survive," she finished.

Fred stood up and began pacing the floor. "First Mario, now Eddie, goddamn it, this is not right! It's just not right!"

Ted also stood up, as did the Deputy. She couldn't blame McKuen for his reaction, it was totally understandable. "Mr. McKuen, Mr. Knowlton, I'm just so very sorry to have to bring you this news. The best thing to do is for everybody to pray for Eddie, that he will come out of this. I have to go now but I will call you later today. Um, also, do you have ... can you give me any information on Eddie's next of kin? Is he married?"

"No, no, he's not married," said Fred. "He ... he lives with his mom. He lives in an apartment downstairs from his mom. He's got his parents, his sister ... I don't know who else."

Dammer drew out her notepad and a pen. "Is his mother's last name Fitzgerald also?"

"I ... no ... I don't know," Fred said. "Her name, geez, you know what, I really don't remember, right now. His father, his father's name is Ed. Ed Fitzgerald, the same as Eddie." Fred suddenly looked shocked. "Oh my god," he said, "no, I can't, how can I call and say, and say, what if he doesn't make it, what if I have to call his parents and say that? Oh my God," he repeated, walking out of the room. Dammer and Knowlton heard the lobby door open and close after him. She looked at the chair he'd vacated; Fred hadn't taken his jacket.

"This is pretty terrible," said Ted. "You have to excuse Fred, he's just so upset. Nothing like this has ever happened to our ski group before. The worst thing up until now, someone broke their leg one year. You know, the thing with Mario yesterday, which was a really bad accident, and then Eddie on top of that, and they were, I mean they are, like, his best friends. So you have to excuse him."

"Don't worry Mr. Knowlton," Dammer replied, "I understand. And it's perfectly all right. But I assure you that Eddie will have the best possible care at St. John's. Let's pray for him, for a positive outcome."

"Thank you Deputy. Thank you very much." Ted extended his hand and she grasped it with both of hers.

"I will phone you later," she said.

Ted nodded. He walked her to the lobby door. They both looked out the window but Fred was nowhere in sight. Ted watched as she got into her vehicle and started the engine. As he turned around he saw that Mackenzie was staring at him from the front desk.

"It's bad news?" she asked softly.

He told her what the deputy had related. They both were silent for a few moments.

"I'll be in my room," he said, turning away.

* * *

11:30 a.m., January 20, 2013. Emergency Room, St. John's Medical Center, Jackson, Wyoming. Dr. Steeler, attending physician: "The patient was brought immediately to the trauma room, where he was exposed and removed from the wet clothing and cold backboard onto the cot. He was immediately insulated with warm blankets. We were unable to intubate the patient given his clenched jaw, but he was bagging easily with a nasal trumpet that had been placed in the field, and we continued to bag-valve mask the patient. It was noted that he did have moderate chest rise with respirations. The patient had no palpable pulse, but a femoral stick was able to obtain blood, which was immediately sent for an arterial blood gas and a stat potassium to help determine whether or not the patient may have a chance at being resuscitated. His initial temperature was noted to be extremely cold as mentioned at 66.6 rectally. However, it does demonstrate the severity of the patient's hypothermia. The patient's initial cardiac rhythm on the Lifepak 12 here was noted to be asystole with no intrinsic activity. The patient's initial pH was returned at 7.1, and his initial potassium was returned at 5.3, both inside the range where resuscitation may be possible if there was no other cause for death.

A bedside ultrasound performed, however, demonstrated no discernible cardiac activity and Doppler failed to show any flow. The patient had received IV access at this point, and a femoral cordis was placed. Please see the separate Procedure Notes for this. Warm fluid resuscitation had been begun while we were awaiting the laboratory results. After the laboratory results were returned, I again reviewed the patient's cardiac activity on ultrasound and noted that he had no intrinsic activity. We were actually considering calling the patient [declaring the patient deceased] when it was noted that on the monitor he did have a very small evidence of electrical activity at a rate of approximately 30 to 40 beats per minute in both lead II and lead I. With the patient's laboratory values being inside the range that resuscitation may be possible at [this] point, it was decided to begin resuscitation and rewarming of the patient. The patient had a bladder temperature probe placed which demonstrated the patient had a temperature of 20.5 Celsius. The patient then had warm bladder irrigation started as well as a left-sides 24 chest tube was placed for thoracic cavity warm fluid lavage. Please see separate Procedure Note for placement of the chest tube. As the patient had no discernible cardiac activity or evidence of Doppler flow through the heart, cardiopulmonary resuscitation was initiated. Shortly after the initiation of cardiopulmonary resuscitation, it was noted the patient had lost all cardiac electrical activity that we had been monitoring. I had discussed the patient with Eastern Idaho Regional Medical Center, and we were making arrangements to transfer the patient there for evaluation by their cardiothoracic surgeon and intensivist for possible rewarming. The patient, however, at that time was noted to have no electrical cardiac activity. We continued cardiopulmonary resuscitation for approximately an hour, and it was noted the patient had asystole throughout this time period."

"At this point, it was required that we have fixed wing transport of the patient to Eastern Idaho Regional Medical Center secondary to

weather. Given the technical difficulty with this, we did elect to recheck the patient's blood work given that he had been demonstrating asystole throughout this period. It was noted that a 2nd arterial blood gas demonstrated a pH of 6.8, and his 2nd potassium was over 9. At this point, I felt that the likelihood of successful resuscitation on this extremely hypothermic patient was significantly low enough that resuscitation efforts could be terminated. The team was consulted and concurred with this. At 1323 hours, the patient was pronounced. The patient was subsequently discussed with the coroner. I did personally notify the patient's mother, Gail McCall [sic] in New York, by phone as well as the leader of his tour group, Ted Nalton [sic]. Our social worker is attempting to help with arrangements for the family."

* * *

"It's a shame," said one of the ER nurses to an orderly. "What was he, 46? He seemed to be in good physical shape, too."

"I was listening to the police radio last night," the orderly replied. "For some reason they called the search off around midnight. They knew he was down in the canyon though."

The ER nurse looked puzzled. "If they knew he was there, why didn't they go get him?" she asked.

"Don't know." He shrugged.

* * *

"People who are lost may experience differing types of reactions. They may panic, become depressed or suffer from 'woods shock.' Panic usually implies tearing around or thrashing through the brush, but in its earlier stages it is less frantic. Most lost people go through some of the stages.... . Regardless of how well and healthy a person seems to be when rescued, there is almost always some degree of shock. Even people who, while lost, appeared to use good judgment with no suggestion of overt panic, exhibit what we

like to call 'woods shock.' ... Undoubtedly, the psychological trauma of being lost will affect behavior ... Remarkably few individuals build a fire or erect a good shelter to protect themselves from the elements." —William G. Syrotuck, Analysis of Lost Person Behavior, pp. 11-12

Ted switched off his cell and placed it on the nightstand in his room at the Parkway Inn. He was a fireman and used to dealing with emergency situations, but this one had hit quite close to home. He had never been pals with Eddie, but wouldn't have wished this for him, or for anyone. Getting lost in the wilderness in the dead of winter, being out there all night, alone, and probably pretty scared. Ted thought about what he himself might have done if he'd been in Eddie's shoes.

First of all, if he had realized he might be spending the night out there, he'd probably have built himself a snow cave or some kind of shelter. Something that would protect him from the wind, and hopefully keep him hidden from bears or other predators. He wasn't sure, but he had heard there were also mountain lions or something roaming around in these parts. He always carried a knife with him, and a lighter, so he'd be able to build a fire for warmth, which might also signal the Search and Rescue team. But as far as he knew, Eddie didn't carry any supplies with him.

He also didn't know why Eddie hadn't used his cellphone, why he didn't make any more calls after he reached 911, but Ted suspected that its battery had died. Everyone in the ski group had complained how spotty the cell coverage was on the mountain. A cellphone continually searching for a signal would deplete the battery much faster.

In any event, if he himself had been stranded out there he was certain he would not have met the same fate. Eddie's clothes were frozen because they had gotten wet. That meant he'd probably been wandering around and fell into that creek they said was at the bottom of the canyon. Ted wouldn't have wandered around.

He would have built a shelter and stayed put till daylight. There wasn't any sense in roaming around in the dark. Why did Eddie do that? He wasn't stupid. Didn't talk much, but it seemed like he had a brain at least. There definitely was something wrong with him though. When he did talk, he had kind of a weird way of speaking. And he was very awkward—except when he was on skis, then he seemed normal.

No one had ever mentioned it, but it seemed to Ted that Eddie could be autistic. If he did have some sort of neurological condition, it might have affected his actions. It could have made him think or act in a different way. That's why he had mentioned to the Ski Patrol the previous night that he thought Eddie was autistic.

And another thing—Eddie wore glasses. Ted knew for a fact that Eddie couldn't see well without them. At one of the ski group gatherings one year, everyone was testing each other's eyesight, jokingly, while they were knocking back a few beers (except for Eddie, who always drank Coca Cola). Eddie was pretty sightless without his specs. What if Eddie had lost his glasses out there— then he would be virtually blind, especially in the dark.

Ted shook his head. It was a shame. But shit happens. He got up from the edge of the bed and slipped his cell into his pocket. Then he went down the hall to Fred's room and knocked on the door. There was no response. Ted stood there for a minute or so before he turned to leave. Just then Fred opened the door. He looked like pure crap, as if he hadn't slept in days, although some of that might be attributable to the amount of Scotch he'd been consuming ever since Mario had broken his leg.

"Come in," Fred said in a hoarse voice. He went to the window side of the room and sat down on the armchair while Ted seated himself on the sofa. They looked at each other for a few moments, without speaking.

"I just got the phone call from the hospital," said Ted.

"Is he gone?"

Ted nodded. Fred closed his eyes and Ted saw a tear rolling down the side of his face.

"I don't understand how this happened, Ted," Fred said, his voice wavering. "It's like some mess of bad luck just came and swooped over us. What did I do? It was just supposed to be a normal ski trip, like we always have."

Ted looked around the room. There were two beds; Fred had been rooming with his nephew Freddie, but he was not there at the moment. The bedclothes were disheveled and there were open suitcases on the luggage stands, and several articles of clothing strewn about the room. On the shelf by the TV there was an empty bottle of Scotch and a few cups, and an ice bucket sitting in a ring of water that was dripping slowly onto the carpet.

"It wasn't your fault, Fred," he said.

"Maybe it was. I think maybe it was my fault. I didn't do a head count on the bus."

"There was so much confusion, Fred. People switched buses because of Mario getting picked up from the hospital—"

"I know, but..." Fred picked up a cup from the coffee table, but it was empty. "He was my friend. I should've noticed he wasn't there. He was my friend."

"Look. You can't blame yourself for this. Eddie skied out of bounds and got lost. You had no control over that. When he found out he was lost, he should have built himself a shelter instead of wandering around in the woods. Christ."

"I have to call his mother," said Fred.

"Maybe someone from the hospital or the Sheriff's Office already called her."

"It doesn't matter. One of us has to call her. Her name's Gail. I remembered. Someone from the ski group has to call her. Like you called her last night to tell her he was lost." He looked at Ted imploringly.

"You want me to call her, don't you," asked Ted.

Fred nodded. "Please."

"Don't worry, I'll take care of it." Ted turned to leave, then looked back at Fred. "Maybe you oughta lay off the booze for awhile. It's not gonna help at this point." He left the room and started to walk to his own room but ran into Larry on the way.

"Hey, Ted," said Larry. "Have they found him?"

Ted paused. "He died, Larry."

There was silence for a few moments. Larry felt his knees give way slightly. He reached out his hand to an antique table in the hallway to steady himself. "Why? What, why?" he stammered. "What happened?"

"He apparently fell into a creek and got wet," Ted replied slowly. "So, once he got wet, he couldn't keep himself warm. He couldn't survive the night. I know he was your good friend, I'm sorry. I just told Fred."

Larry nodded. "Okay. Thanks." He turned around and went downstairs. He took the side exit out, he didn't want to go through the lobby. He couldn't face seeing other people yet. He had to take some time to let this sink in. He stood just outside the door, gazing into the gray Wyoming winter day until his body felt as numb as his mind. He, Fred and Mario had been Eddie's closest friends. He hadn't told Mario that Eddie was missing, the guy had enough troubles. But now it was unavoidable. *This has truly become the vacation from hell.*

* * *

Mario: "I didn't speak to no one. I wasn't speaking to any of my friends except Larry that stayed with me. He goes on trips, but he doesn't ski. He goes sightseeing, this and that, you know. But he stayed with me throughout the whole trip, helped me to the bathroom and so on and so forth... I didn't want to speak to no one ... Even two, three weeks after we came back I didn't want to talk to anyone ... If I didn't break my leg, I would have noticed right away Eddie missing. You understand? I would have noticed Eddie right away missing. No who, no what, no whatever, because my first thought was always Eddie. You know, is Eddie here, you know. I would have known that Eddie was missing, he is not on the bus."

* * *

At the South Leigh Canyon trailhead, the snowmobile road is less than a hundred yards from South Leigh Creek. Walking into the woods to the accompaniment of the westward-flowing current, one comes face to face with a bunch of fallen trees and the remnants of an old wooden bridge with only one retaining wall on the embankment remaining.

Eddie "Cola" Fitzgerald had been found lying face down in the snow, less than a mile from the parking area. He would have been following the creek's current, knowing that the creek, in its turn, would follow gravity and flow downward. At some juncture, he could have expected there would be a road, a house, a sign of civilization.

If only the moon had not been so possessive with its sliver of light that night. If only Eddie had known that just on the other side of the creek was the road for which he'd been searching. If only Idaho SAR, or Wyoming SAR, or anybody, had taken the initiative to go down this road with snowmobiles that night.

One could imagine a parallel universe in which Eddie, cold and exhausted, crosses the creek at its lowest point and climbs up the embankment to the road. He follows the road in the same direction as the stream, and after another mile or so, he sees the cream-colored house with the pickup truck in the driveway. Or a different parallel universe in which Mark Silver tells searchers that Eddie is near a stream. Or one in which Mario doesn't break his leg. Or one in which the rope line at the North Boundary Traverse had never been taken down. Or one in which someone on the ski group bus says "Hey, where's Eddie?" Or ...

* * *

Hank Storm put down the newspaper and stared out the window at the starry Wyoming sky. "You know, Grace," he said to his wife, "There's something wrong with this story." Hank was a journalist for the Driggs local paper, and an expert skier and snowmobiler. He knew that mountain as well as anyone alive.

"What do you mean?"

"Well, according to this article," he gestured at the paper on the table, "Don Oscar said that skier who died had ducked a rope at Grand Targhee. But I know there's no rope there to duck. Don's excuses for why Search and Rescue waited till the next day to go get him don't hold water either. The whole thing just doesn't sit right. Someone dropped the ball here. Bad. Maybe more than one person. The guy's family deserves to know what really happened to him."

Grace Storm knew there'd be no peace in their home until Hank figured out the truth of the story. She'd seen that look in his eyes before. "What are you going to do?" she asked.

"First, I'm going to call up my colleague, Ann, in New York. Send her to the guy's funeral. Have her talk to his family."

"You need to be careful," Hank's wife reminded him. "Those big ski resorts have a lot of political power. Maybe you should let this one go. Stay out of it."

Hank looked at her. "Honey, how can you even suggest that to me? Everything points to major negligence being committed here, and someone *died* because of it."

Hank went over to the desk and flipped the Rolodex to his colleague's name while their toddler son tugged on his pants.

"Hank?" his wife entreated him. "I don't want to tell you what to do, but just think about this for a minute. If you open up a can of worms in Wyoming—if there's a big scandal—there's going to be lawsuits. And some very powerful people are going to be mad, and they might come after *you*, if you break the story. It happens to journalists all the time!" She reached for their son and hugged him to her, and tousled his brown curly hair.

Hank sighed. "Grace. If it was *our* son who went off on a ski trip ..."

Grace held his gaze for a moment. "You're right," she said finally. "I'm sorry. Your decision."

Hank found his colleague's business card in the Rolodex, and extracted it. He stood for a moment with the card in his hand, flexing it back and forth nervously. He knew that once he made this phone call, and asked Ann to speak with the family of the dead man, the wheel of fate would begin turning in a direction he wouldn't be able to reverse. He had a responsibility to ensure the safety of his family, yes. But as a journalist, he also had a responsibility to his community. If people at Grand Targhee or Search and Rescue had not done their job, they were letting the community down, and it was his job as a journalist to report on it. But this wouldn't be like covering the town council meeting, or Youth Club Soccer. This story was potentially huge.

Hank felt the need for some fresh air, and went out the back door to stand on the porch for a few moments. He breathed deeply, inhaling the Wyoming winter atmosphere and gazing up at the stars. Should he pursue the story, or not?

Suddenly, a meteor plunged to earth in a bright arc, surrounded by the blackness of space dotted with distant stars. Hank smiled. He went back inside the house and pulled the business card out of his pocket. He picked up the phone and dialed the New York number.

Epilogue

Gail McCaul, Eddie's mother: "I'm so fearful about lying there in bed and having those thoughts about him, that I now pray. I never prayed. I had to get a book out to find out what prayers to say. I made up my own to talk to God, to my God. I don't know if there's a God; I'm hoping there is. And I pray. I talk to Eddie at night. That's what I do. I tell him things, and I tell him to help Christine in her life. Actually talking to Eddie ... when I'm talking, I can't think, so it helps. I can't think about that cold black night. That's all."

On January 22, 2010, two days after Eddie "Cola" Fitzgerald's death, Mandy Jones was called in by Grand Targhee administration to amend her incident report because it was "too emotional." She agreed to do so, but kept a copy of her original report.

One week after Eddie's death, a meeting was held at Grand Targhee which was attended by Grand Targhee administration, ski patrollers, Teton County law enforcement personnel and Search and Rescue personnel who had participated in the search for Eddie. It was agreed that Wyoming henceforth would always respond with "boots on the ground" to any search taking place in Wyoming, and not rely solely on telephone communication.

On Feb. 4, 2010, an After Action Report was presented by Captain Brett Ferry of the Teton County Wyoming Sheriff's Dept. In his findings he noted "Unfortunately, this incident is fraught with mistakes. The 'perfect storm' reference made by Clay Striver perhaps is the accurate description."

A memorial service for Eddie was held in Long Island. His mother Gail told the funeral home to expect around 20 people. Between 75 and 100 showed up, including most of the members of the Long Island Ski Group. They brought two large placards containing collages of photos and hand-written reminiscences.

A new mail carrier was appointed to Eddie's mail route in Queens, New York. Eddie's customers were shocked and upset to learn of his death. Some of them cried.

Two weeks after Eddie's death, Grand Targhee reinstated the rope line at the North Boundary Traverse.

Mandy Jones' contract as Grand Targhee Ski Patroller was not renewed. (She was, however, invited to rejoin the staff of the ski school.) She left Wyoming and signed on as a ski patroller in an Alaska resort.

In November of 2010 Pete Kerry resigned from his position as Ski Patrol Director. The position was filled by Assistant Ski Patrol Director Jon Alexander.

In 2011 Brett Montague resigned from his position as General Manager of Grand Targhee.

In 2011 Eddie's mother Gail lost Sam, her partner of seventeen years, to congestive heart failure.

In 2011 the new Teton County Wyoming SAR building, with helicopter hangar, was completed.

In 2011 Don Oscar was divorced from his wife. He moved to Victor, Idaho, where Clay Striver and helicopter pilot Len Jameson also lived.

In 2012 Terry Diamond resigned from his position as Search and Rescue Commander for Teton County Idaho.

In 2012 Clay Striver was killed in a helicopter crash while undertaking a search and rescue mission. Pilot Len Jameson and an additional SAR team member were severely injured.

In 2012 Grand Targhee settled out of court in a wrongful death lawsuit brought by the Fitzgerald family.

In 2013, the Teton County Wyoming Sheriff's Dept. fired Don Oscar from his position as Search and Rescue Coordinator "for cause." Oscar no longer holds any position with Search and Rescue.

Mario's broken leg healed just fine without surgery. He gave up skiing.

Appendix I

Main Characters

Long Island Ski Group:
Eddie "Cola" Fitzgerald
Fred McKuen, founder
Freddie, Fred's nephew
Ted Knowlton (aka "Norton", "Naughton", "Knowington", "Nalton"), LISG liaison with Search and Rescue
Kathryn Sherlock, member
Larry Andersson, member
Mario, member
Rich & Cheryl, members
Marco, member
Ross, member

Grand Targhee:
Jon Alexander, Assistant Ski Patrol Director
Jesse O' Leary, lead patroller
Mandy Jones, ski patrol
Jared, ski patrol
Andrew, ski patrol
Cathy, ski patrol
Bill Redmond, ski patrol

Kris Hart, ski patrol
Gary Thibault, Ski Patrol Incident Investigation Supervisor
Brett Montague, Grand Targhee General Manager

Teton County Wyoming Search & Rescue:
Don Oscar, Coordinator
Clay Striver
Tom Catalin
Len Jameson, helicopter pilot

Teton County Wyoming Sheriff's Dept.
Sheriff Jim Jennings
Deputy Dina Dammer

Teton County Idaho Search & Rescue:
Terry Diamond, Commander
Jesse O'Leary, member (also Targhee Ski Patroller)
Dan Van Horst, member
Jack & Bev Stills, members

Teton County Idaho Sheriff's Dept.
Mark Silver, 911 dispatcher
Viola Walls, 911 supervisor
Sharon Courier, 911 dispatcher
Tesha Wilson, 911 dispatcher
Sheriff Lichevy

The Fitzgerald family:
Eddie "Cola" Fitzgerald
Ed Fitzgerald, Sr.
Christine Fitzgerald, Eddie's sister
Gail McCaul, Eddie's mother

Others:
Gabe Mender, ER nurse, Driggs hospital
Dr. Steeler, St. John's Medical Center, Jackson

Appendix II

Glossary of Ski Terms

Beacon: See "transceiver"

Bluebird: Nice weather

Fall Line: Most direct path down the slope, following gravity

GPS: Global Positioning System, a device that detects its location using various means such as UTM or Latitude-Longitude coordinates

Incident Command System or ICS: Also known as NIMS, National Incident Management System. Organizational system used by rescue personnel in emergency situations

Milk Run: The first run of the day

Mogul: Mounds of snow, either natural or made by skiers' repeated turns in the same places on the slope

MP: Missing Person

Off Piste: Un-groomed area of the resort

Post-Holing: Walking in deep snow

Pow: Short for 'powder', fresh, light, dry snow

Probe: Multi-sectioned aluminum pole that can extend to several feet, for locating avalanche victims buried beneath the snow

Skins: Thin layers made of nylon or mohair that clip onto the tips and tails of the skis, providing the traction necessary for the skier to re-ascend the mountain without the aid of a ski lift

Snowcat: Bulldozer-like machine used to groom trails or transport skiers and their gear

Snowplow: Slowing down or stopping on skis by pointing tips inward and putting pressure on the inside edges

Transceiver: Also known as a 'beacon,' a device that emits a pulsed radio signal which rescuers use to locate someone buried by an avalanche.

Trail Indicators: Green circle (the easiest trails at a ski resort)
Blue Square (more difficult)
Black Diamond (the most difficult)

Traverse: Moving in a direction perpendicular to the fall line; a groomed trail leading to an adjacent area in the resort

UTM: Universal Transverse Mercator System, whereby the earth is divided into rectangular sections with corresponding alphanumeric indicators

Wave Off: Ski patroller's signal that all is well

About the Author

Susan Tatarsky began her writing career as a ghostwriter for technical articles appearing in scientific trade journals. Her writing developed in tandem with her career as a professional musician, and she has been a regular contributor to music industry publications. She was an avid backcountry Nordic skier until she gave up skiing to save her knees for kung fu. She holds eight USKSF Championship Tournament gold medals.

CPSIA information can be obtained at www.ICGtesting.com
Printed in the USA
BVOW02s1315310515

402569BV00003B/165/P